Guided Math Lessons in Fifth Grade

Guided Math Lessons in Fifth Grade provides detailed lessons to help you bring guided math groups to life. Based on the bestselling *Guided Math in Action*, this practical book offers 16 lessons, taught in a round of 3—concrete, pictorial and abstract. The lessons are based on the priority standards and cover fluency, word problems, fractions, and decimals. Author Dr. Nicki Newton shows you the content, as well as the practices and processes, that should be worked on in the lessons so that students not only learn the content but also how to solve problems, reason, communicate their thinking, model, use tools, use precise language and see structure and patterns.

Throughout the book, you'll find tools, templates and blackline masters so that you can instantly adapt the lesson to your specific needs and use it right away. With the easy-to-follow plans in this book, students can work more effectively in small guided math groups—and have loads of fun along the way! Remember that guided math groups are about doing the math. So throughout these lessons, you will see students working with manipulatives to make meaning, doing mathematical sketches to show what they understand and can make sense of the abstract numbers. When students are given the opportunities to make sense of the math in hands-on and visual ways, then the math begins to make sense to them!

Dr. Nicki Newton has been an educator for over 30 years, working both nationally and internationally with students of all ages. She has worked on developing Math Workshop and Guided Math Institutes around the country; visit her website at www.drnickinewton.com. She is also an avid blogger (www.guidedmath.wordpress.com), tweeter (@drnickimath) and Pinterest pinner (www.pinterest.com/drnicki7).

Also Available from Dr. Nicki Newton

(www.routledge.com/eyeoneducation)

Guided Math Lessons in Kindergarten:
Getting Started

Guided Math Lessons in First Grade:
Getting Started

Guided Math Lessons in Second Grade:
Getting Started

Guided Math Lessons in Third Grade:
Getting Started

Guided Math Lessons in Fourth Grade:
Getting Started

Day-by-Day Math Thinking Routines in Kindergarten:
40 Weeks of Quick Prompts and Activities

Day-by-Day Math Thinking Routines in First Grade:
40 Weeks of Quick Prompts and Activities

Day-by-Day Math Thinking Routines in Second Grade:
40 Weeks of Quick Prompts and Activities

Day-by-Day Math Thinking Routines in Third Grade:
40 Weeks of Quick Prompts and Activities

Day-by-Day Math Thinking Routines in Fourth Grade:
40 Weeks of Quick Prompts and Activities

Day-by-Day Math Thinking Routines in Fifth Grade:
40 Weeks of Quick Prompts and Activities

Leveling Math Workstations in Grades K—2:
Strategies for Differentiated Practice

Daily Math Thinking Routines in Action:
Distributed Practices Across the Year

Mathematizing Your School:
Creating a Culture for Math Success
Co-authored by Janet Nuzzie

Math Problem Solving in Action:
Getting Students to Love Word Problems, Grades K-2

Math Problem Solving in Action:
Getting Students to Love Word Problems, Grades 3–5

Guided Math Lessons in Fifth Grade

Getting Started

Dr. Nicki Newton

Routledge
Taylor & Francis Group

NEW YORK AND LONDON

Cover image: © Getty Images

First published 2023
by Routledge
605 Third Avenue, New York, NY 10158

and by Routledge
4 Park Square, Milton Park, Abingdon, Oxon, OX14 4RN

Routledge is an imprint of the Taylor & Francis Group, an informa business

Library of Congress Cataloging-in-Publication Data
Names: Newton, Nicki, author.
Title: Guided math lessons in fifth grade : getting started / Dr. Nicki Newton.
Description: First edition. | New York, NY : Routledge, 2022. |
Identifiers: LCCN 2022003894 (print) | LCCN 2022003895 (ebook) | ISBN 9780367770754 (hbk) | ISBN 9780367760038 (pbk) | ISBN 9781003169666 (ebk)
Subjects: LCSH: Mathematics—Study and teaching (Elementary)
Classification: LCC QA135.6 .N4855 2022 (print) | LCC QA135.6 (ebook) | DDC 372.7/044—dc23/eng20220525
LC record available at https://lccn.loc.gov/2022003894
LC ebook record available at https://lccn.loc.gov/2022003895

ISBN: 978-0-367-77075-4 (hbk)
ISBN: 978-0-367-76003-8 (pbk)
ISBN: 978-1-003-16966-6 (ebk)

DOI: 10.4324/9781003169666

Typeset in Palatino
by Apex CoVantage, LLC

Contents

Acknowledgements

This book is dedicated to my parents, my grandparents and my family. I also dedicate this series to my professor Lin Goodwin, who had a huge influence on how I teach and what I believe about education. I also thank Dan at www.brainingcamp.com for allowing me to use the screenshots of the phenomenal virtual tools!

Meet the Author

Dr. Nicki Newton has been an educator for over 30 years, working both nationally and internationally, with students of all ages. Having spent the first part of her career as a literacy and social studies specialist, she built on those frameworks to inform her math work. She believes that math is intricately intertwined with reading, writing, listening and speaking. She has worked on developing Math Workshop and Guided Math Institutes around the country. Most recently, she has been helping districts and schools nationwide to integrate their State Standards for Mathematics and think deeply about how to teach these within a Math Workshop Model. Dr. Nicki works with teachers, coaches and administrators to make math come alive by considering the powerful impact of building a community of mathematicians who make meaning of real math together. When students do real math, they learn it. They own it, they understand it and they can do it. Every one of them. Dr. Nicki is also an avid blogger (www.guidedmath.wordpress.com), tweeter (drnickimath) and Pinterest pinner (www.pinterest.com/drnicki7/).

Dr. Nicki Newton, Educational Consultant
Phone: 347–688–4927
Email: drnicki7@gmail.com

Find More Online!

Resources, videos and conversations with Dr. Nicki can be found at Routledge as well as in the Guided Math Dropbox Resources: https://bit.ly/2Ja4sMY

1
Introduction

Figure 1.1 Guided Math Example 1

There is a group of students who are really struggling with dividing a whole number by a fraction. I pull them to work on building the concept with pattern blocks. They come, and we work with fraction pattern blocks so we have more denominators. I ask them to model this story: *Aunt Mary baked 2 pies. She cut them into sixths. How many pieces did she get?*

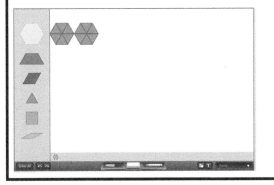

www.brainingcamp.com

Figure 1.2 Guided Math Example 2

Another group of students decided that they wanted to meet and talk about dividing fractions by whole numbers. We explore this through storytelling. I tell them there is half of a pizza left. *Four friends split half a pizza. What fraction of the pizza did they each eat?* They work it out with the fraction strips. They figure out that if they divided that 1/2 of the pizza between 4 people that they would each get 1/8 of the pizza each.

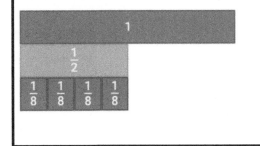

www.brainingcamp.com

Guided math is a small-group instructional strategy that teaches students in their zone of proximal development around the priority standards. There are so many standards, but every state has priority focus standards. Those are the standards that you teach in a small guided math group. It is a time for hands-on, minds-on learning based on the standards. It is a time for discussing ideas, listening to the thinking of others, reasoning aloud and becoming confident, competent mathematicians.

Guided math groups are for everyone! Too often, students are rushed through big ideas, understandings and skills. They are left with ever-widening gaps. Guided math groups give teachers the time needed to work with students in a way that they can all learn. Guided math groups can be used to close gaps, teach on-grade-level concepts and address the needs of students who are working beyond grade level.

Guided math groups can be heterogeneous or homogeneous. It depends on what you are trying to do. If you are teaching a specific skill, such as dividing fractions, and one group is still

DOI: 10.4324/9781003169666-1

◆ 1

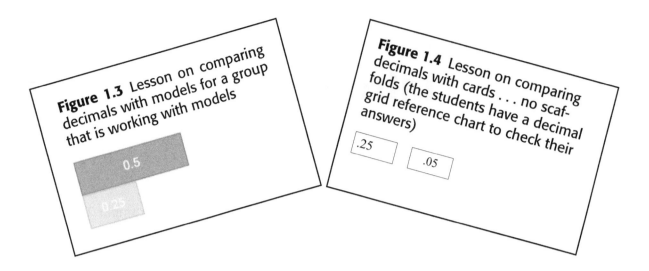

Figure 1.3 Lesson on comparing decimals with models for a group that is working with models

0.5

0.25

Figure 1.4 Lesson on comparing decimals with cards . . . no scaffolds (the students have a decimal grid reference chart to check their answers)

.25

.05

struggling with the idea, you could continue working with manipulatives to model the problem. You could also pull a different group that understands the concept and work with them at an abstract level, playing a bingo or jeopardy game. The groups are flexible, and students work in different groups at different times, never attached to any one group for the entire year. Students meet in a particular guided math group three or four times based on their specific instructional needs, and then they move on. Other times, the students all work together in a heterogeneous group exploring different ideas.

Guided math groups can occur in all types of classrooms. Typically, they are part of a math workshop. In a math workshop (see Figure 1.5) there are three parts

Opening	**Student Activity**	**Debrief**
♦ Energizers and Routines	♦ Math Workstations	♦ Discussion
♦ Problem-Solving	♦ Guided Math Groups	♦ Exit Slip
♦ Mini-Lesson		♦ Mathematician's Chair Share

What Are the Other Kids Doing?

The other students should be engaged in some type of independent practice. They can be working alone, with partners or in small groups. They could be rotating through stations based on a designated schedule, or they could be working from a menu of must-dos and can-dos. The point is that students should be practicing fluency, word problems and place value and working on items in the current unit of study. This work should be organized in a way that students are working in their zone of proximal development (Vygotsky, 1978).

Differentiating workstations helps purposefully plan for the learning of all students. For example, the fluency workstation games should be divided by strategy; for example, students can be working on building basic fact power or working on multidigit numbers, depending on what they need (Baroody, 2006; Van De Walle, 2007; Henry & Brown, 2008). Another example is word problems. Students should be working on all the different types of word problems. Knowing the learning trajectory and understanding the structures that go from simple to complex can help organize the teaching and learning of word problems (Carpenter, Fennema,

Figure 1.5 Math Workshop

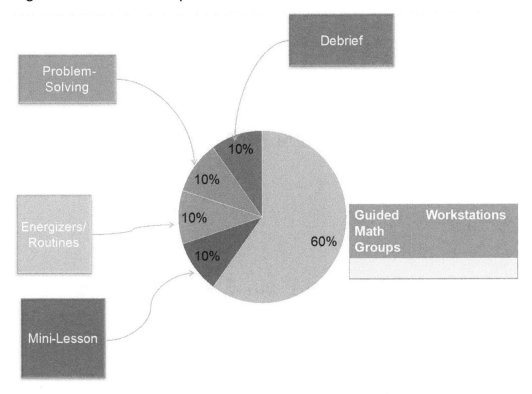

Franke, Levi, & Empson, 1999, 2015; Fuchs, Zumeta, Schumacher, Powell, Seethaler, Hamlett, & Fuchs, 2010); Jitendra, Hoff and Beck (1999).

Benefits of Guided Math Groups

♦ See student knowledge in action.
♦ Monitor the concepts and skills that are understood.
♦ Catch and address the misunderstandings.
♦ Ask questions that highlight thinking.
♦ Analyze thinking.
♦ Listen to conversations.
♦ Assess in the moment.
♦ Redirect in the moment.
♦ Differentiate as needed.

Key Ideas

♦ Different Reasons: remediate, focus on grade-level topics or work beyond grade level
♦ Cycle of Engagement: concrete, pictorial and abstract
♦ Heterogeneous and Homogeneous Grouping
♦ Math Workshop
♦ Math Workstations
♦ Benefits of Guided Math

Figure 1.6 Workstation Contract

Workstation Contract

I have the privilege of learning with the Math Workstations.

I will play fair.

I will be a good sport. When I win, I will celebrate appropriately. When I lose, I'll be a good sport.

I will use the math manipulatives the way they are supposed to be used.

I will use the digital resources the way they are supposed to be used.

I will put everything back neatly.

I will work hard every day.

I will keep trying when the going gets tough!

My Signature:_____

Date:_____

Summary

Guided math is a great way to differentiate learning for all your students. Focus on the priority standards. Students approach these standards through a concrete, pictorial and abstract cycle of engagement. Sometimes, the groups are homogeneous groups and other times the groups are heterogeneous. Guided math groups can be done in a variety of ways, either in a traditional setup or a math workshop model. The other students should always be doing work that they are familiar with and are practicing in the math workstation. Many times, the work that students are working on in the guided math group is carried over into the math workstation. When the students are in guided math groups, the other students should be meaningfully engaged in math workstations. All of this works together to give all students a chance to learn.

Reflection Questions

1. How are you differentiating instruction around the priority standards right now?
2. Currently, how do you group students? What informs your grouping?
3. Do you have a plan to make sure that everybody fully understands the priority standards?

References

Baroody, A. J. (2006). Why Children Have Difficulties Mastering the Basic Number Combinations and How to Help Them. *Teaching Children Mathematics*, 13, 22–32.

Carpenter, T. P., Fennema, E., Franke, M. L., Levi, L., & Empson, S. B. (2015). *Children's Mathematics: Cognitively Guided Instruction*. Portsmouth, NH: Heinemann.

Fuchs, L. S., Zumeta, R. O., Schumacher, R. F., Powell, S. R., Seethaler, P. M., Hamlett, C. L., & Fuchs, D. (2010). The Effects of Schema-Broadening Instruction on Second Graders' Word-Problem Performance and Their Ability to Represent Word Problems with Algebraic Equations: A Randomized Control Study. *Elementary School Journal*, 110(4), 446–463. Retrieved on January 4, 2020, from https://www.ncbi.nlm.nih.gov/pubmed/20539822.

Henry, V., & Brown, R. (2008). First-Grade Basic Facts: An Investigation into Teaching and Learning of an Accelerated, High-Demand Memorization Standard. *Journal for Research in Mathematics Education*, 39(2), 153–183.

Jitendra, A. K., Hoff, K., & Beck, M. M. (1999). Teaching Middle School Students with Learning Disabilities to Solve Word Problems Using a Schema-Based Approach. *Remedial and Special Education*, 20(1), 50–64. https://doi.org/10.1177/074193259902000108.

Van de Walle, J. A., & Lovin, L. A. H. (2006). *Teaching Student-Centered Mathematics: Grades 3–5*. Boston: Pearson.

Vygotsky, L. S. (1978). *Mind in Society: The Development of Higher Psychological Processes*. Cambridge, MA: Harvard University Press.

2

Behind the Scenes

Assessment

Assessment is a crucial element in designing a guided a math lesson. Teachers have to know where their students are along the trajectory of learning so that they can plan to teach them purposefully. Teachers need actionable data. Actionable data is data that can be used immediately to develop meaningful lessons. At the beginning of the year, teachers need to get data about the priority standards/major cluster standards from the year before so they can figure out if there are any gaps and make a plan to close them. Richardson notes that "[t]he information gathered from the assessments helps teachers pinpoint what each child knows and still needs to learn. They are not about 'helping children be right', but about uncovering their instructional needs" (n.d.).

Remember every summer, students lose 2.6 months of math at least (Shafer, 2016). Teachers should assess fluency, word problems, operations and algebraic thinking and place value at the beginning of the year. In the middle of the year, teachers should assess all the grade-level work done in these areas during the first part of the year. At the end of the year, teachers should assess all the priority standards for the grade. Throughout the year, teachers should rely on entrance and exit slips, quizzes, anecdotals, unit assessments and conferring to get information about students (see Figure 2.1).

Figure 2.1 Exit Slip Example

25 × 4	12 × 12
347 × 9	45 × 50

Circle the easy problems. Underline the tricky ones. How do you feel about multiplication?

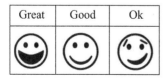

Great	Good	Ok

DOI: 10.4324/9781003169666-2

Grouping

Guided math groups should have between 3 to 5 students. There are basically 3 ways to decide on groups. One way is to pull students by their readiness needs. Another way is to give the *students the opportunity to choose* what they want to meet and do in groups. The teacher can give the students a list of choices. A third way is to brainstorm possibilities about what interests them and then let them decide what they want to explore more deeply. Groups should last between 10 and 15 minutes. Remember the attention span rule: Age plus a few minutes.

Differentiation

After teachers get the data, they need to use them for differentiation (see Figure 2.2). Some of the work is to close the gaps. In guided math groups teachers should be accelerating the learning (meaning addressing the standards that students are struggling with and connecting them to the grade level standards. Also, teachers should be extending learning for students who understand the topic. Some of the work is to teach in the grade-level zone. A big part of the differentiation aspect of guided math lessons is the concrete, pictorial and abstract cycle. Sometimes, students know the answer but do not necessarily understand the math. It is crucial to do quick assessments with students to make sure that they understand the math. For example, students might know the procedure for multiplying fractions but not be able to explain the concept. We would practice it in a variety of ways with manipulatives, with sketches and with the numbers. We would also have the students to verbalize what they are doing and contextualize it by telling stories (NCTM, 2014).

Figure 2.2 Differentiation

Group 1: Tell me a story about ½ of a ¼ and solve it with models.	Group 2: Tell me a story about ½ of a ¼ and solve it with math sketches.	Group 3: Explain how to multiply fractions.
$\frac{1}{4}$ $\frac{1}{8}$	$\frac{1}{4}$ $\frac{1}{8}$	When you multiply fractions, you are looking for a piece of a piece. You multiply the numerators and the denominators.

Types of Groups

When we are thinking about grouping, it is about meeting the needs of the students where they are and taking them to the next level of what they need to learn at that grade. Students are emerging in their learning along the continuum. It is about creating flexible groups that students can move through as they work on different concepts. These groups should never be "fixed" and track students throughout the year. They are temporary, flexible, focused groups that teach students what they need when they need it, and then students move on to different work (see Figure 2.3).

Figure 2.3 Types of Groups by Readiness

Group 1: Emergent	Group 2: Early Fluent	Group 3: Fluent	Group 4: Advanced Fluent
These are the students that are working below grade level. They often have many gaps and misunderstandings. It is important to work on closing gaps as well as highly scaffolding (but not over-scaffolding) current grade-level material.	These students are approaching grade level. They have some gaps and also need acceleration (which is connecting pertinent past standards directly to on grade level work).	These students are right at grade level.	These students are working above grade level. This doesn't mean that the work should be done from the next grade level; however, as Kathy Richardson notes, it is important to go deeper with concepts rather than to jump to the next ones.
Students can be emergent learners in one area and advanced, fluent learners in another. These are not meant to be labels that stick with students all year. As Dr. Kim Reid always said, "Labels are for boxes." Although we need a way to describe how students are doing in particular areas, we must never categorize them with fixed labels. Students move and develop along their own trajectory. With the appropriate scaffolding, we can teach everybody and move them toward achieving grade-level standards. Guided math groups are part of the kidwatching and responsive teaching cycle of learning.			
Rather than viewing some children as "low" or "behind" or "lacking in skills," kidwatching teachers view all children as creative, capable learners—on their way to "achieving control over the conventions of [math]—always 'in process,' always moving forward" (Flurkey, 1997, 219; Owocki & Goodman, 2002, preface).			

Rotations

Teachers can assign students to where they are going to go, visiting different stations every day. Another way to do it is to give the student a menu for the week with can-dos and must-dos. Either way, students should do fluency, word problems and place value and work from the current unit of study.

Standards-Based

Every guided math lesson should be centered around priority standards. There are so many standards to teach, so we have to focus. We have to get in there, dig deep and discuss ideas so that students can learn them. When students sit down in the group, the first thing the teacher should talk about is the work they are going to be doing for the day. The *I can or I am* learning to statement should be up, and students should discuss what they are going to be learning and what the criteria of success for that learning will look like. There is an ongoing discussion about whether to say *I can or I am* learning to. *I can* is more of a statement about what students will be able to do in the future. *I am* learning to speaks more to the continuum of learning and allows for students to be at different places along that continuum.

Dixon points out that sometimes, we shouldn't tell the students the I can statement at the beginning all the time because then you in essence tell the ending of the story before it begins (2018a). This is an excellent point; it depends on where you are at in the concept and skill cycle and what the lesson of the day is. If you are trying to get students to explore and wonder about something, then don't upfront it, but discuss it at the end after they have explored the topic. However, if you are working on something that you have been doing for a while, you can say, "Today we are going to continue looking at . . ."

Depth of Knowledge

Guided math lessons are about building depth of knowledge with students. They should reach a variety of levels, not just level one activities. For example, instead of just telling stories, teachers should ask questions such as "The answer is 1/5. What is the question?" Instead of just giving the students an equation to solve, teachers should also say things like "Give me 2 different ways to make 2/10." We want students to be reasoning about numbers in a variety of ways, using as many scaffolds as they need to become confident and competent.

Scaffolding

Scaffolds are a fundamental part of guided math lessons. There are so many different types of scaffolds. We are going to discuss grouping scaffolds, language scaffolds and tool scaffolds. Grouping scaffolds help students become proficient by having students work with partners and in small groups before they practice the skill on their own. This is the social aspect of grappling with the content. Oftentimes, students learn a great deal from each other through discussions and interactions. In the group, you can partner students up and watch them play the game, take notes and ask different questions to guide them as they work together.

Language is often scaffolded with illustrated pictures of the vocabulary and language stems on sentence strips. Dixon (2018b) talks about how at the beginning of learning, a concept that it can be productive for students to have to explain the topic without the "cover" of the vocabulary, meaning that sometimes students will use words but not understand the concepts; their lack of understanding can be hidden by the use of the correct vocabulary. If they don't have that, then they have to explain the math. In later lessons, when students understand the math, then it's okay to upfront the vocabulary.

Scaffolding is so important and yet we have to be really careful not to over-scaffold and as Dixon warns to also avoid "just in case" scaffolding (2018c). We want to help students as they need it, but we do not want to steal the struggle. Students need the opportunity to engage in the productive struggle, but it should not be an unproductive struggle (Hiebert & Grouws, 2007; Blackburn, 2018). There is a very careful balancing act that teachers conduct when scaffolding in a guided math group.

In the guided math group, teachers should make sure that tools are part of the learning cycle. In planning to unpack the concepts and skills in small groups, teachers should think about the ways in which students can wrestle with topics concretely, pictorially and abstractly. There should also be an emphasis on verbalization and contextualization (NCTM, 2014). The magic of the manipulatives is the conversation and the activities that are done along with them. Students need to reflect on and explain the concepts and how the manipulatives are being used to model those concepts. In a small group, students should be doing the math and exploring and discussing the ideas as they use the manipulatives (Ball, 1992; Baroody, 1989; Bruner, 1960; Burns, n.d.).

Engagement

Engagement is important. Research links engagement to students' *affect*—their feelings and emotions about learning (Mcleod, 1992 cited in Ingram). We find that students' engagement is shaped by the sociocultural environment in which they are learning. This environment is created by how they are constructing knowledge together through discussions, activities and the norms of learning (Op 't Eynde, 2004; Boaler & Greeno, 2000; Greeno, Collins, & Resnick, 1996). The interactions that students have in small guided math groups are very important. It helps shape students' mathematical identities—who and what they see themselves as in terms of a mathematician.

We find that students are engaged when they participate in strong lessons in a strong community. A strong lesson has a clear purpose, is relevant and makes sense to their lives; it is brain-friendly and flows easily, allowing them to quickly get into a "good 'work-flow'" and dive deep into the material (Claflin, 2014). The strong community of learners in essence means that "they got each other's back!" Everybody is in it to win it with each other. Students are helpful, trusting, risk-taking and comfortable. In the small group, they should be willing to try things out and be assured that it is not always going to work the first time and that they might not get it even the second time around but that with perseverance, they can learn it.

Another really important aspect of working with students is the wonder of learning. The guided math table is a special experience. I like to have guided math journals and special pencils and toolkits for students to work with at the table. Students look forward to coming to the guided math group. Often, I use dice, dominos, cards and board games. Since the same structure can be used, the students are ready to work on the content, meaning that if we play bingo, then students know that structure, so they can immediately focus on the content. I might play a decimal bingo game with one group and watch another group of students play tic-tac-toe with each other.

Student Accountability

While the students are working in math workstations, they should be filling out different sheets of the work they are doing (see Figures 2.4 and 2.5). They should be recording what they are doing. Some sheets record everything that students are doing. Other games have students record only some of their work.

> The most important thing about math workshop is that you organize it well from the beginning. You must do the first 20 days. In the first 20 days you teach the students how to work in the workshop. Here is a resource for that: www.drnickinewton.com/downloads/.

Students have to learn how to work independently before you start pulling them in guided math groups. The premise of Math Workshop is that all students can work on their own productively before you start working with them in small groups.

There are two key elements to a good workstation. The first is a clear goal for the workstation. Students need to know what the math is and how they are going to work on that math and what it looks like when they are actually learning that math. The second is that they have an accountability system so that they know the teacher will be monitoring their work.

Figure 2.4 Student Recording Sheet Example 1

Comparing Decimals		
Roll the dice. Record your roll. Compare with the symbols. Whoever has the highest decimal wins a point. Whoever gets 5 points first wins the round. Whoever wins 3 rounds wins the game.		
Partner 1	**< = >**	**Partner 2**
.41	>	.22

Figure 2.5 Student Recording Sheet Example 2

Recording Sheet: Board Game
When I went around the board, I solved several multiplication problems.
I solved:
$\frac{1}{2} \times \frac{1}{4} = \frac{1}{8}$
$\frac{1}{3} \times \frac{1}{3} = \frac{1}{9}$
$\frac{1}{6} \times \frac{1}{2} = \frac{1}{12}$
The important thing to remember about multiplying fractions is. . . .
That you multiply the numerators and the denominators.

Key Ideas

♦ Assessment
♦ Grouping
♦ Differentiation
♦ Rotations
♦ Standards-Based
♦ Depth of Knowledge
♦ Scaffolding
♦ Engagement
♦ Student Accountability

Summary

The key to great guided math groups is assessment. When you have great assessments, then you can group appropriately for differentiation that matters. Lessons should be standards-based. Teachers must always plan for the level of rigor in the lesson. Lessons should be scaffolded with language supports, tools, templates and student grouping. All the other students must be accountable for the work they are doing in the workstations. Engagement is necessary.

Reflection Questions

1. What specific assessments do you have around the priority standards?
2. In what ways are you evaluating your lessons for rigor?
3. In what ways are you scaffolding lessons?
4. How do you know that the students are on task and learning in the math workstations?

References

Ball, D. L. (1992). Magical Hopes: Manipulatives and the Reform of Math Education. *American Educator: The Professional Journal of the American Federation of Teachers*, 16(2), 14–18, 46–47.

Baroody, A. J. (1989). Manipulatives Don't Come with Guarantees. *Arithmetic Teacher*, 37(2), 4–5.

Blackburn, B. (2018). Retrieved on January 5, 2020, from www.ascd.org/ascd-express/vol14/num11/productive-struggle-is-a-learners-sweet-spot.aspx.

Boaler, J., & Greeno, J. G. (2000). Identity, Agency, and Knowing in Mathematical Worlds. In J. Boaler (Ed.), *Multiple Perspectives on Mathematics Teaching and Learning* (pp. 171–200). Westport, CT: Ablex Publishing.

Bruner, J. S. (1960). On Learning Mathematics. *The Mathematics Teacher*, 53(8), 610–619.

Burns, M. (n.d.). How to Make the Most of Manipulatives. Retrieved on August 28, 2016, from http://teacher.scholastic.com/lessonrepro/lessonplans/instructor/burns.htm?nt_id=4&url= http://store.scholastic.com/Books/Hardcovers/Harry-Potter-and-the-Chamber-of-SecretsThe-Illustrated-Edition-Book-2?eml=SSO/aff/20160429/21181/banner/EE/affiliate/////2–247765/&affiliate_id=21181&click_id=1707726852.

Claflin, P. (2014). Retrieved on January 20, 2020, from www.theanswerisyes.org/2014/12/08/student-engagement-checklist/.

Dixon. (2018a). Retrieved on January 4, 2020, from www.dnamath.com/blog-post/five-ways-we-undermine-efforts-to-increase-student-achievement-and-what-to-do-about-it/.

Dixon. (2018b). Retrieved on January 4, 2020, from www.dnamath.com/blog-post/five-ways-we-undermine-efforts-to-increase-student-achievement-and-what-to-do-about-it-part-4-of-5/.

Dixon. (2018c). Retrieved on January 4, 2020, from www.dnamath.com/blog-post/five-ways-we-undermine-efforts-to-increase-student-achievement-and-what-to-do-about-it-part-3-of-5/.

Greeno, J. G., Collins, A. M., & Resnick, L. B. (1996). Cognition and Learning. In D. C. Berliner & R. C. Calfee (Eds.), *Handbook of Educational Psychology* (pp. 15–46). London: Prentice Hall International.

Hiebert, J., & Grouws, D. A. (2007). The Effects of Classroom Mathematics Teaching on Students' Learning. In F. K. Lester Jr. (Ed.), *Second Handbook of Research on Mathematics Teaching and Learning* (pp. 371–404). Charlotte, NC: Information Age.

McLeod, D. B. (1992). Research on Affect in Mathematics Education: A Reconceptualization. In D. Grouws (Ed.), *Handbook of Research on Mathematics Teaching and Learning* (pp. 575–596). New York: NCTM and Macmillan.

National Council of Teachers of Mathematics. (2014). *Principles to Actions: Ensuring Mathematical Success for All*. Reston, VA: Bergen University.

Op 't Eynde, P. (2004). A Socio-Constructivist Perspective on the Study of Affect in Mathematics Education. In M. J. Hoines & A. B. Fuglestad (Eds.), *28th Conference of the International Group for the Psychology of Mathematics Education* (Vol. 1, pp. 118–122). Bergen, Norway: Bergen University College.

Owocki, G., & Goodman, Y. M. (2002). *Kidwatching: Documenting Children's Literacy Development.* Portsmouth, NH: Heinemann.

Shafer, L. (2016). Summer Math Loss. Why Kids Lose Math Knowledge, and How Families Can Work to Counteract It. Retrieved on January 15, 2019, from www.gse.harvard.edu/news/uk/16/06/summer-math-loss.

3

Architecture of a Small-Group Lesson

There are suggested components of a small-group lesson. All the components are essential. However, you will do things in different ways depending on the lesson. Every small-group lesson should begin with an introduction to the lesson. In this introduction, students should talk about what they are going to work on that day. Sometimes, the teacher even writes it up on the board, like an agenda, so students know what to expect. The teacher usually writes the general outline of the lesson and what the goals are for the lesson. The teacher then goes over the "I am learning to" statement as well as what it looks like when students can actually do that skill or understand that concept (criteria for success). However, sometimes this is done at the end instead of the beginning. After students have explored a topic, they then discuss what they learned, and they name it.

After the opening, everyone could talk about the math vocabulary and phrases that are associated with the current topic, or this could wait and be done at the end of the lesson too. At some point, the teacher should discuss the vocabulary because math is a language and students should understand the words they are using. Then the lesson begins with either a discussion, an exploration or an activity. The teacher might model it or might just jump into the topic. Oftentimes, the teacher will ask the students to give their input about the topic before they begin. After a time of exploration, the students will begin to further explore the topic, either on their own, with a partner or with the whole small group.

At the end, the teacher will lead the debrief. This is where the students will discuss what the math was for the day, as well as how they practiced that math. They should also talk about how they feel they are doing with that math. This is the part of the lesson where students are reflecting and monitoring their process and progress. They talk about the parts of the topic that are easy and the parts that are "tricky." Language is important, so instead of saying difficult or hard, I tend to say "tricky, fuzzy or climbing." Using a mountain metaphor can help students explain their journey. I explain to students that they could be just looking at the mountain from the base (preparing for a great adventure), climbing but not at the top yet (enjoying the climb), almost at the top or at the top (whereby they can say it's sunny on the summit). Planning is key (see Templates 3.1–3.7).

Introduction

Agenda

- ♦ I Am Learning to/I Can
- ♦ Vocabulary/Language Frames
- ♦ Launch by Teacher
- ♦ Student Activity (alone/pairs/group)
- ♦ Teacher Observes, Questions, Facilitates Learning and Takes Notes

  DOI: 10.4324/9781003169666-3

♦ Wrap-Up/Reflection
♦ Next Steps

Planning and Preparation

There are many different ways to keep a system of organization. Binders work well. Have a guided math toolkit where the teacher keeps all the games, manipulatives, activity sheets and assessments that are needed for each lesson. Keep lesson plans, anecdotal notes and observation checklists in this folder. Also, have a guided math folder for each child to keep all their work in it. This comes in really handy during parent conferences. There are many different template examples below (see Templates 3.1–3.7).

Figure 3.1 Quick Plan

Week:	Assessments	Workstations
Big Idea:	Entrance Slips:	Group 1
Enduring Understanding:	Exit Slips:	Group 2
Essential Question		Group 3
I am learning to . . .		Group 4

Figure 3.2 Guided Math Planning Sheet

Guided Math Planning Sheet	
Launch	
Model	
Checking for Understanding	
Guided Practice/ Checking for Understanding	
Set Up for Independent Practice	

Figure 3.3 Guided Math Groups Planning Template 1

Guided Math Groups	
Big Ideas: **Enduring Understandings:** **Essential Questions:** **Vocabulary:** **Language Frames:**	**Cycle of Engagement:** **Concrete, Pictorial, Abstract** **Depth of Knowledge Level:** **1 2 3 4** **Standard/I can statement:**
Group 1:	Group 2:
Group 3:	Group 4:

Figure 3.4 Guided Math Planning Template 2

Guided Math Lesson Plan: Group:		
Week: Big Idea: Enduring Understanding:	Standard: I can/I am learning to Statement:	Vocabulary: Language Frame: Materials:
Lesson: Intro: Guided Practice: Individual Practice: Sharing: Debrief:		
Comments/Notes: Next Steps:		

Figure 3.5 and 3.6 Guided Math Planning Templates 3 and 4

Guided Math Lesson				
Big Ideas: **Enduring Understandings:** **Essential Questions:**	**Vocabulary:** **Language Frame:**	**Standard:** I can/I am learning to . . . Concrete/Pictorial/Abstract		
Depth of Knowledge Level: 1 2 3 4	**Goal:** ♦ Remediate ♦ Teach ♦ Dive Deeper	**Materials/Tools**		
		dice	Board games	Unifix cubes/ bears/tiles
		dominos	counters	base ten blocks
		deck of cards	calculators	pattern blocks
		white boards/ markers	gm journals	geoboards
Beginning of the Lesson	**Guided Practice**	**Independent Practice**		
Assessment/ Exit Slip	**Discussion**	**Questions**		
Comments/Notes: **Ahas:** **Wow:** **Rethink:** **Next Moves:**				

Guided Math		
Group: Week:		
Big Idea: Enduring Understandings: Essential Questions:	Vocabulary: Language Frame: DoK Level: 1 2 3 4	Lessons: 1st 2nd 3rd
Content Questions:		
Name	What I noticed	Next Steps

Figure 3.7 Guided Math Planning Template 5

Unit of Study: Big Idea: Enduring Understanding: Standard:		Essential Question: Vocabulary: Language Frame: I Can Statement:		
	Group 1:	Group 2:	Group 3:	Group 4:
Monday	Lesson: Materials: DoK Level: Concrete/ Pictorial/ Abstract	Lesson: Materials: DoK Level: Concrete/ Pictorial/ Abstract	Lesson: Materials: DoK Level: Concrete/ Pictorial/ Abstract	Lesson: Materials: DoK Level: Concrete/ Pictorial/ Abstract
Tuesday	Lesson: Materials: DoK Level: Concrete/ Pictorial/ Abstract	Lesson: Materials: DoK Level: Concrete/ Pictorial/ Abstract	Lesson: Materials: DoK Level: Concrete/ Pictorial/ Abstract	Lesson: Materials: DoK Level: Concrete/ Pictorial/ Abstract
Wednesday	Lesson: Materials: DoK Level: Concrete/ Pictorial/ Abstract	Lesson: Materials: DoK Level: Concrete/ Pictorial/ Abstract	Lesson: Materials: DoK Level: Concrete/ Pictorial/ Abstract	Lesson: Materials: DoK Level: Concrete/ Pictorial/ Abstract

Note: DoK = Depth of Knowledge

It is also important to have forms to collect notes as you watch student work. Figure 3.8 is an example.

Figure 3.8 Anecdotal Recording Form

Anecdotal Notes

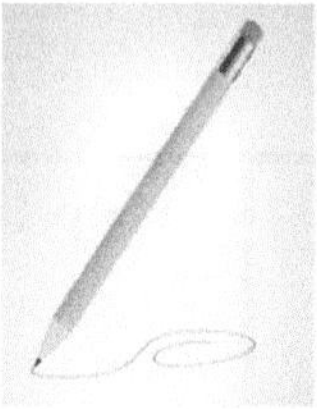

What did you see? 	What did you hear? 	What do you think? 	What questions do you have? 
Student	Student	Student	Student
Student	Student	Student	Student

Having reflection sheets for students to think about the work they are doing is important (see Figure 3.9).

Figure 3.9 Reflection Sheet

Keeping parents in the loop is very important (see Figure 3.10).

Figure 3.10 Parent Letter

Dear Parent/Guardian,

We are learning how to _____.

Today during our guided math group I noticed that _____ struggled with this skill/concept.

I am sending home this activity/game so that you can work with _____.

Please call, email me or write a letter if you have a question.

Thank you for helping with this!

Sincerely,

Figure 3.11 Celebration Certificate

Celebration Certificate

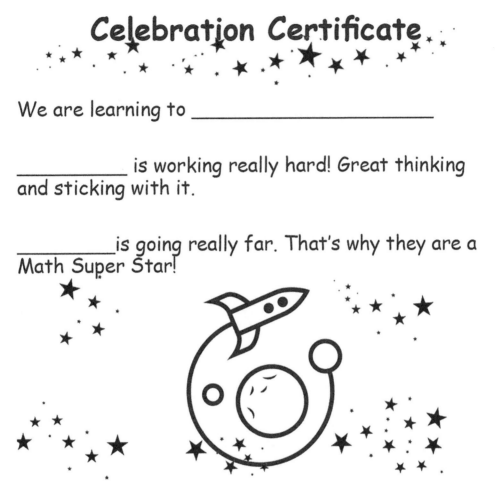

We are learning to _____

_____ is working really hard! Great thinking and sticking with it.

_____ is going really far. That's why they are a Math Super Star!

Key Points

♦ Architecture of the Lesson
  ◦ I Am Learning to/I Can
  ◦ Vocabulary/Language Frames
  ◦ Launch by Teacher
  ◦ Student Activity (alone/pairs/group)
  ◦ Wrap-Up
  ◦ Next Steps

♦ Planning Templates
♦ Anecdotal Recording Sheet
♦ Parent Letter
♦ Celebration Letter

Summary

There is a suggested architecture for small guided math groups. Teachers must plan for the learning goal, the vocabulary supports, the tools, the launch of the lesson, the students practicing the math and the wrap-up and next steps. All these elements are important parts of the lesson. They all contribute to the success of the guided math group. Using planning templates with these elements on them helps teachers plan for each of the elements.

Reflection Questions

1. Do your guided math lessons have all the elements in them?
2. What types of templates are you currently using for guided math groups?
3. What is an element that you need to focus on in the architecture?

4

Talk in the Guided Math Group

One of the most important things that happen in the guided math group is the discussion. We have to teach students to be active participants and engaged listeners. We want students to learn to respect each other deeply and seek to truly understand each other without judgment. They have to learn to develop and defend their thinking, justify their answers and respectfully disagree with each other. The National Council of Teachers of Mathematics (NCTM) defines *math talk* as "the ways of representing, thinking, talking, and agreeing and disagreeing that teachers and students use to engage in [mathematical] tasks" (NCTM, 1991).

Questions

It is so important to ask good questions. The questions should reach beyond the answer. As Phil Daro notes, we have to go "beyond answer-getting." The questions in the guided math group should be designed to get students to understand more fundamentally the mathematics of the grade level. Good questions don't just happen; they are planned for. The teacher should know ahead of time the types of questions that they will ask and why they will ask them. In the plan for the lesson, the teacher should brainstorm some possible questions that push students' thinking. These are not yes-or-no questions but rather ones that require students to explain themselves, show what they know and defend and justify their thinking (see Figure 4.1).

DOI: 10.4324/9781003169666-4

Figure 4.1 Planning for Great Questions

Before the Lesson	During the Lesson	After the Lesson
Plan what you want to get your students to think about. The tasks that we choose will determine the thinking that occurs.	**Observe, monitor and note what is happening in the group. Checklists, sticky notes and anecdotal note structures work well here.**	**Reflect, assess and decide what's next.**
How will you go about that? What questions will you ask them?	What is your data collection system during the lesson?	What did you see? What did you hear?
How will you set them up to actively listen and productively participate?	Scaffold student questioning?	What did the students do? What do you need to do next?
How will you get them to engage with the ideas of others?	Scaffold student-to-student interactions?	What instructional moves will you make? What pedagogical moves will you make?
How will you get them to offer detailed explanations of their own thinking using numbers, words and model?		
Plan for misconceptions. How will you address them and redirect students?		

When students are sitting in that group, they should be having an engaging experience that builds mathematical knowledge and skills. At the table, students should be encouraged to actively participate. They should be thinking aloud, sharing their thoughts, analyzing and critiquing the thoughts and actions of others and taking risks throughout the explorations. We should always be thinking about the levels of rigor of the conversation that the students are engaged in (see Figure 4.2).

Depth of Knowledge

In terms of rigor, there are 4 levels of questions.

Figure 4.2 Depth of Knowledge (DoK) Questions

DoK 1	DoK 2 **At this level, students explain their thinking.**	DoK 3 **At this level students, have to justify, defend and prove their thinking with objects, drawings and diagrams.**
What is the answer to . . . Can you model the problem? Can you identify the answer that matches this equation?	How do you know that the equation is correct? Can you pick the correct answer and explain why it is correct? How can you model that problem in more than one way? What is another way to model that problem? Can you model that on the . . . Give me an example of a . . . type of problem. Which answer is incorrect? Explain your thinking.	Can you prove that your answer is correct? Prove that . . . Convince me that . . . Show me how to solve that and defend your thinking.

*Level 4 is more strategic project-based thinking.

It is very important to include open questions as part of your repertoire at the guided math table. Here is an example: The answer is 2 1/2. What is the question?

Although you will ask some questions that require students to remember a fact or show you that they can do a skill, your questions must extend beyond this level. You should be focusing on questions that have more than one answer or way of solving the problem.

Questions That Pique Curiosity

Your questions should pique curiosity. They should lead students into further explorations. They don't have to be answered immediately. Students should have a sense of wonder. There should be some "Aha" moments, some "Wow" moments and some "I don't get it" moments. For example, "What if we didn't have addition?" "Tell me 3 situations in which you would use subtraction." "Why is multiplication important in real life?"

Scaffolding Questions for English Language Learners

Students should understand the questions being asked. The language should be accessible, and everyone should have a way to enter into the conversation. When thinking about instruction with English Language Learners (ELLs), we must consider the type of language support they will need (https://mathsolutions.com/math-talk/; http://fspsscience.pbworks.com/w/file/fetch/80214878/Leveled_20Questions_20for_20ELLs;www.aworldoflanguagelearners.com/asking-answering-questions-with-ells/). Oftentimes, they will need help with syntax and sentence structure, so it is important to scaffold these into the conversation. Give students an opportunity to refer to language stems, use language bookmarks, write down and/or draw the answer (see Figure 4.3).

Figure 4.3 Scaffolding ELL Questions

Low levels of support: (advanced language learners; levels 3 & 4)	Moderate levels of support: (developing language learners; level 2)	High levels of support: (emerging language learners; level 1)
Use a word bank (illustrated): Explain how they did that? Explain your thinking? Explain your model/ strategy? What are 2 ways you could model your thinking? Can you describe your thinking? Can you show us what you did? Can you describe how you did it? Can you explain what they did? Why is that true? Why is that not true? Explain how you did it. Decide if they are correct?	Use a sentence frame: I got the answer by _____. How can you use ____ to help you solve _____? How can you model that? What is the name of that strategy? (mini-anchor chart) How did you do that? Why did you use that model/strategy? How did they do that? Is it this or that? Which strategy did you use? (visual support)	Allow students to draw/ write the answer: Point to the . . . Show me your answer . . . Which is the best answer? What is the name of that strategy? Do you see it here? (mini-anchor chart of strategies) Give students a model sentence and a sentence frame: How did you get the answer? How did you _____? Do you agree? Yes or no? Show me the _____. Point to the _____. Circle the ____. Can you point to the strategy you used?

Adapted from http://fspsscience.pbworks.com/w/file/fetch/80214878/Leveled_20Questions_20for_20ELLs www.aworldoflanguagelearners.com/asking-answering-questions-with-ells/

Although these are structures for ELLs, they are great question types to consider with the various students you are working with. They are also great ways to think about scaffolding questions for special education students.

Probing Questions

Teacher questions, as well as student-to-student questions, should provide insight into student thinking. During the guided math lesson and after it, the teacher should jot down what they have learned about students' thinking, about students' knowledge and how they are making sense of the math they are learning.

Student-to-Student Conversations

It is crucial that the teacher sets up a discussion in which students are asking each other questions. They could have question rings, bookmarks, mini-anchor charts or other scaffolds to help them ask each other questions (see Figures 4.4 and 4.5). In these conversations, one of the things that students are doing is listening to each other and comparing what they did.

Figure 4.4 Question Bookmark

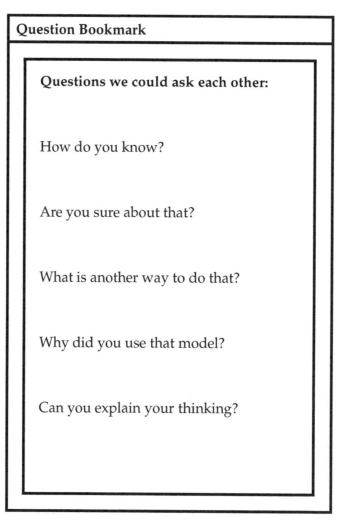

Question Bookmark

Questions we could ask each other:

How do you know?

Are you sure about that?

What is another way to do that?

Why did you use that model?

Can you explain your thinking?

Figure 4.5 Talk Cards/Talk Ring

I agree because...	I disagree because...	I need some time to think.	Why is that true?

Are you sure?	Do you agree or disagree?	Can you think of another way?	I'm confused still.

Yes I'm sure because

No, I'm not sure. I'm thinking about it.

Way 1
Way 2

Figure 4.6 5 Talk Moves Poster

5 Talk Moves Poster				
Revoice	Restate	Reason	Wait Time	Group Participation
I heard you say . . .	Who can say what was said in your own words?	Are you sure? Can you prove it?	Give me a few seconds	Who wants to add to that?

5 Talk Moves and More

The idea of having a framework for how students engage with each other is very important. Chapin, O'Connor, and Anderson (2009) theorized this framework around 5 talk moves: revoicing, restating, group participation, reasoning and wait time. There are also other really helpful frameworks (Kazem I & Hintz,2014; O'Connell & O'Connor, 2007). In the section that follows, we will explore how some of these can help us structure the discussions in guided math groups. Oftentimes, these structures are used together; for example, a teacher might ask someone to restate what someone said and then encourage the group to add on (see Figures 4.7–4.11).

Figure 4.7 Revoicing

What It Is	What It Does	What It Sounds Like
The teacher restates in the words of the student what they just said.	This allows the student to hear back what they said, the other students to hear and process what has been said and everyone to think about it and make sure they understand it. This teaches students the power of hearing what they have said and trying to make sense of it.	*So you said . . . Is that correct?* *Let me make sure I understand, you are saying . . .* *So first you . . . and then you . . .* *So you used this model?* *So you used this strategy?*

Figure 4.8 Restating

What It Is	What It Does	What It Sounds Like
The teacher or other students restate in their own words what has been said. Students then verify what has been said by checking it with the original student.	This allows the student to hear back what they said, the other students to hear and process what has been said and everyone to think about it and make sure they understand it. This requires that students listen and pay attention to each other so they can restate what has been said. This teaches students how to listen to each other and make sense of what their peers are saying.	*Who can restate what Susie just said?* *Who can tell in their own words what Jamal just said?* *Who can explain what Carol meant when she said . . .*

Figure 4.9 Reasoning

What It Is	What It Does	What It Sounds Like
Teachers and students are asking each other for evidence and proof to defend and justify what they are saying.	This requires students to engage with each other's thinking. They must compare, contrast, justify and defend their thinking with the other group members. This teaches students the power of defending and justifying their thinking with evidence and proof.	*Why did you do that?* *Is that true?* *Why did you use that strategy?* *Can you prove it?* *Are you sure?* *How do you know?* *Why did you use that model?* *Does that make sense?* *Do you agree or disagree, and why or why not?* *How is your thinking like Tom's?* *Is there another way?*

Figure 4.10 Group Participation

What It Is	What It Does	What It Sounds Like
Students write down or model their thinking and then share it with the whole group.	This allows students to focus on their own strategies and models, jot them down and then share them. This teaches students the power of justifying and defending their thinking.	*Use a model to show . . .* *Illustrate your strategy.* *On your white boards, show us . . .* *In your guided math journal, show your thinking with numbers, words or pictures. Be ready to share it with the group.*

Figure 4.11 Wait Time

What It Is	What It Does	What It Sounds Like
Teachers and students give each other 20–30 seconds of uninterrupted time to think, write or draw about what they are doing. This is done after the question is asked and then when the answer is given. Students should be given the time to think about the answer and then respond to it.	This allows students the time to gather their thoughts, clarify their thinking for themselves and just time to think. It gives more people time to process what is happening. It teaches them the power of stopping to think instead of rushing into a conversation.	*Okay, now I am going to ask some questions, but I want you to take some think time before you answer.* *Terri just gave an answer. Let's think about what she just said before we respond.* *Show me with a silent hand signal when you are ready.* *Let's give everyone some time to think about this.* *Is everybody ready to share, or do you need more time? Show me with a hand signal.*

It is very important to use different talk moves with students during guided math group in order to scaffold the discussions. The previously discussed structures can definitely get you started doing this. It is important to plan for what you want to work on so that it isn't just random conversations. You should be explicit with students when teaching these structures. For example, you might say, "Today we are working on wait time. I want you to think about giving each other the time to think as we talk. Remember, just because you are ready, doesn't mean your neighbor is yet." There are other ways to facilitate discussions in groups. Let's take a look at these (Figures 4.12–4.16).

Figure 4.12 Making Connections

What It Is	What It Does	What It Sounds Like
The teacher and students are asking each other to make connections with what has been said at the table.	It requires students to listen to each other and think about how what they did connects to what someone else did. This teaches students the power of making connections with each other's thinking.	*How is that the same as what Marta did?* *How is that different from what Joe did?* *This is like what Trini did . . .* *How are these models the same, and how are they different?* *How are these strategies the same, and how are they different?*

Figure 4.13 Partner Talk

What It Is	What It Does	What It Sounds Like
Students talk with their math partners about the math before they share out with the group. They might even draw or write something to share out.	This allows students to think out the math with each other, try to make sense of it and then be able to explain it to the whole group. This teaches students the power of working together to make sense of the math.	*Turn and talk to your partner.* *Tell your partner what you think and why you think that.* *Show and explain to your partner what you did.* *Defend your thinking to your partner.*

Figure 4.14 Prompting Questions

Prompting for Student Participation		
What It Is	**What It Does**	**What It Sounds Like**
The teacher or the students encourage each other to participate in the conversation.	This allows students to participate with each other in the discussion. It openly asks for participation that builds on what has just been said. This teaches students the power of participating in a discussion.	*Who would like to add to that?* *Who wants to say more?* *How did you do it? Was your way the same or different from the way ____ did it?* *Is there another model?* *Is there another strategy?* *Is there another way?*

Figure 4.15 Clarifying Questions

Clarifying One's Own Thinking		
What It Is	**What It Does**	**What It Sounds Like**
The teacher and students take the time to clarify their thinking.	It allows students to expand on their original thoughts. It requires them to give more examples, show more models and explain at a deeper level.	*Can you explain that further?* *Can you tell us more?* *What does that mean?* *Can you show us a model and explain it?* *Can you illustrate your strategy and explain it?*

Figure 4.16 Reflection Questions

Reflecting/Revising/Probing		
What It Is	**What It Does**	**What It Sounds Like**
The teacher and the students take time to reflect on what has been said and possibly revise their thinking.	This gives students an opportunity to rethink about what they have just done. They get permission to change their minds. It teaches them the power of reflecting and revising their work.	*Did anybody change their mind?* *Did anybody revise their thinking?* *Now that you see this model, what do you think?* *Now that you see this strategy, what do you think?* *Thinking about what Jamal just said, how does that help us with our thinking?*

Key Points

- Questions Matter
- Plan for Great Questions
- DoK Questions
- Questions That Pique Curiosity
- Student-to-Student Conversations
- Scaffolding Questions for ELLs
- 5 Talk Moves and More

Summary

Planning matters. We must plan for good conversations. We must think about the ways in which we want our students to engage with each other and then actively do that in our groups. Think about the level of rigor of our questions. Think about what kinds of questions that pique curiosity. How do we get students to engage with each other respectfully, confidently and competently? We must stay conscious of scaffolding our questions for ELLs so that everyone has a way to enter the conversations. We need to consider the different types of talk moves that allow us to have rigorous, engaging and productive conversations.

Reflection Questions

1. What stands out for you in this chapter?
2. What will you enact right away?
3. What questions do you still have?

References

Chapin, S., O'Connor, C., & Anderson, N. (2009). *Classroom Discussions: Using Math Talk to Help Students Learn, Grades K-6* (2nd edition). Sausalito, CA: Math Solutions Publications.

Kazemi, E., & Hintz, A. (2014). *Intentional Talk: How to Structure and Lead Productive Mathematical Discussions*. Portsmouth, NH: Stenhouse.

O'Connell, S., & O'Connor, K. (2007). *Introduction to Communication, Grades 3–5*. Heinemann. Retrieved on November 24, 2020, from https://mathsolutions.com/math-talk/.

Retrieved on November 24, 2020, from http://fspsscience.pbworks.com/w/file/fetch/80214878/Leveled_20Questions_20for_20ELLs.

Retrieved on November 24, 2020, from www.aworldoflanguagelearners.com/asking-answering-questions-with-ells/.

5
Fluency

Fluency is a multidimensional concept. We like to think of it as a 4-legged stool: accuracy, flexibility, efficiency and instant recall (Brownell & Chazal, 1935; Brownell, 1956, 1987; Kilpatrick, Swafford, Findell, & National Research Council (U.S.), 2001; National Council of Teachers of Mathematics, 2000). Although we eventually want students to have instant recall, we need them to understand what they are doing with the numbers first. The emphasis in the guided math group is to do a variety of engaging, interactive, rigorous, student-friendly activities that build a fundamental understanding of the relationship numbers have to each other. As you explore the facts with the students, be sure to do concrete, pictorial and abstract activities with them and constantly making the connections between these 3 things. There should be several ways for students to practice that are fun and challenging. Students should keep track of how they are doing as well.

Basic fact fluency is a major part of third grade. Fourth-grade students should come into the grade having fluency within 100 for multiplication and division and within 1000 for addition and subtraction. In fourth grade, students continue with all 4 operations. With addition and subtraction, students work on fluency within 1 million using traditional strategies. With multiplication and division, they begin to work with multidigit numbers. Fifth-grade students' fluency is the multiplication of 2-digit numbers by 2-digit numbers. However, oftentimes, the basic facts need to be reviewed and firmed up, with special emphasis on learning higher addition and subtraction fact strategies, such as doubles, doubles plus 1 and 2, bridging 10 and half facts. Research says that we should devote at least 10 minutes a day to fluency practice (NCEE, 2009). It should be done as energizers and routines, in workstations and sometimes as guided math lessons. Teachers should integrate fluency work throughout the year because students learn their basic facts at different times and need ongoing practice.

Research Note 🔍

♦ There has been a long debate on traditional fact-based instruction centered on memorization and strategy-based instruction centered on number sense and using strategies. Strategy-based instruction helps students understand the math they are doing and to do it with eventual flexibility, efficiency, automaticity and accuracy (Baroody, Purpura, Eiland, Reid, & Paliwal, 2016; Henry & Brown, 2008; Thornton, 1978).

♦ Boaler (2015) argues that the emphasis of rote memorization through repetition and timed testing is "[u]nnecessary and damaging."

♦ Several scholars have promoted engaging practice through strategy-based games and activities that can scaffold the learning of basic facts (Van de Walle, 2007; Godfrey & Stone, 2013; Kling & Bay-Williams; Newton, 2016; Newton, Record, & Mello, 2020).

DOI: 10.4324/9781003169666-5

In this chapter, we explore the following:

♦ Multiplication Strategies: Doubling and Halving
♦ Division Math Mats
♦ Multiplying Double-Digit Numbers
♦ Division of a 3-Digit Number Divided by a 2-Digit Number

Multiplication Strategies: Doubling and Halving

Figure 5.1 Overview

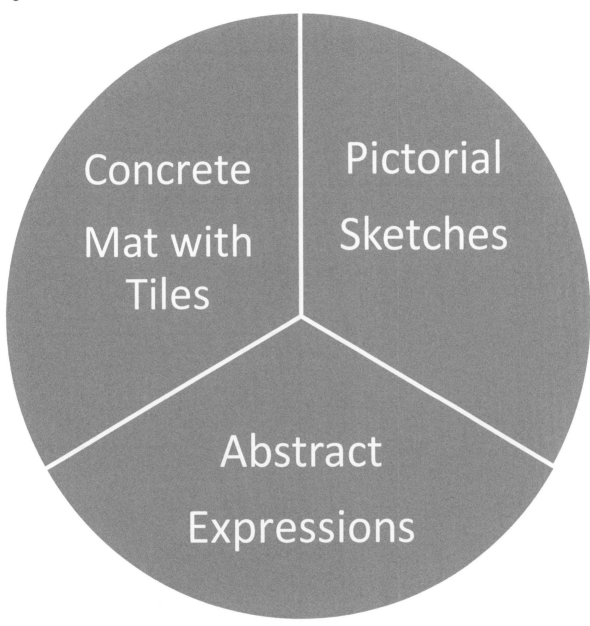

Figure 5.2 Planning Template

Using Doubling and Halving	
Big Idea: Numbers, Operation Meanings & Relationships; Basic Facts & Algorithms **Enduring Understanding:** Students can use different strategies to multiply. **Essential Question:** Why are strategies important? How do they help us to be more efficient? **I can statement:** I can multiply using different strategies.	**Materials** ♦ Paper ♦ Pencils ♦ Manipulatives
	Vocabulary & Language Frames **Vocabulary:** Multiplication, Multiply, Factor, Product **Math Talk:** I used the strategy of . . .
Cycle of Engagement **Concrete:** Halve the rows double amount in each row. $4 \times 6 = 24$ $2 \times 12 = 24$ 	**Math Processes/Practices** ♦ Problem Solving ♦ Reasoning ♦ Models ♦ Tools ♦ Precision ♦ Structure ♦ Pattern
	Pictorial: $2 \times 3 = 1 \times 6$
	Abstract: $5 \times 20 = 10 \times 10$

Figure 5.3 Differentiation

3 Differentiated Lessons
In this series of lessons, students are working on the strategy of doubling and halving. They are developing this concept through concrete activities, pictorial activities and abstract activities. Here are some things to think about as you do these lessons.

Emerging	On Grade Level	Above Grade Level
It is important that students understand the concept by exploring it with smaller numbers that they can do concretely and conceptualize.	Do a lot of work with different manipulatives and have students do math sketches. Also have students really think about different strategies and when it is efficient to do this one.	The next step is to think about ways to enrich the learning. Students who understand the topic and are working above grade level can come up with a project to work on that explores the topic in real life.

 Looking for Misunderstandings and Common Errors

This is a great strategy to do with some problems. It is important that students understand what they are doing and why it works so they don't just think it is a magic trick. Take the time to explore the concept with smaller numbers and manipulatives so that students can see and feel what happens when you double one factor and half the other one.

Figure 5.4 Anchor Chart

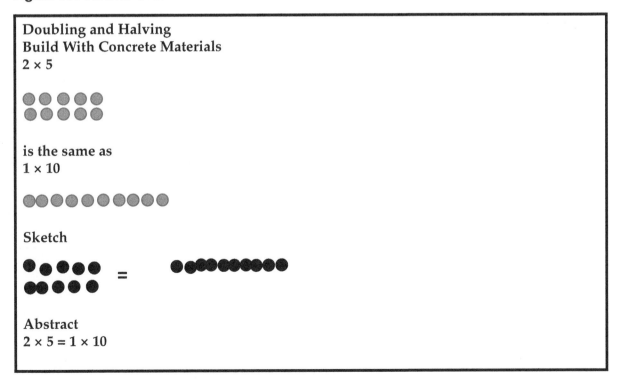

Figure 5.5 Concrete Introduction

	Introduction to Concrete Explorations
Launch	**Teacher:** Today we are going to look at the strategy of doubling and halving. **Vocabulary:** Multiplication, multiplying, factors, products, doubling, halving, strategy, efficient **Math Talk:** I used the strategy of . . .
Model	**Teacher:** We are going to explore what happens when you double one factor and halve the other. Everybody set up 3 × 2. Now double the 3 and halve the 2. What do you see? **Micah:** I see that it is the same amount. **Timmy:** I see where double 3 is 6 and half of 2 is 1.
Checking for Understanding	**Teacher:** Okay, let's explore 2 × 4. **Mary:** I see 1 × 8. I doubled 4 and halved 2. **Teacher:** Okay, so I am going to give each one of you a problem to solve. I want you to solve it any way you want and then explain it back to the group. Model it with your manipulatives.

Figure 5.6 Concrete Student Activity

	Concrete Student Activity	
Guided Practice/ Checking for Understanding	**Teacher:** Who wants to go next? Let's look at 4 × 4. **Charles:** I doubled one of the factors and halved the other. I got 2 × 8. This is the same amount. 
Set Up for Independent Practice	Every child shares their problem and how they solved it. We are going to be talking more about this in the upcoming days. We are going to do this with larger numbers. Are there any questions? What was interesting today? What was tricky?

Figure 5.7 Lesson Close

Close
♦ What did we do today? ♦ What was the math we were practicing? ♦ What were we doing with our tiles? ♦ Was this easy or tricky? ♦ Are there any questions?

Figure 5.8 Doubling and Halving Problem Sets

2 × 4	3 × 2
5 × 2	10 × 2
4 × 4	2 × 2
12 × 2	12 × 4
15 × 4	30 × 4
12 × 12	12 × 10
14 × 15	12 ×16

Figure 5.9 Visual Introduction

Introduction to Visual Explorations

Launch	**Teacher:** Today we are going to look at the strategy of doubling and halving. **Vocabulary:** Multiplication, multiplying, factors, products, doubling, halving, strategy, efficient **Math Talk:** I used the strategy of . . .
Model	**Teacher:** We are going to be sketching out some problems using the strategy of doubling and halving. 4 × 5 **Yesenia:** I see that 4 × 5 can also be 2 × 10. 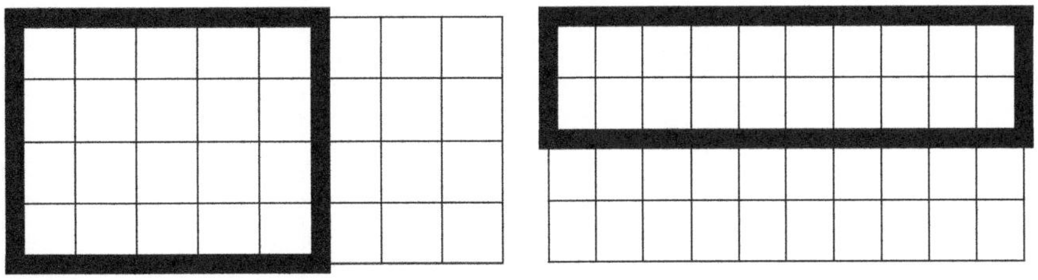
Checking for Understanding	**Teacher:** Listen to this problem: **4 × 6** **Dan:** It can become 8 × 3 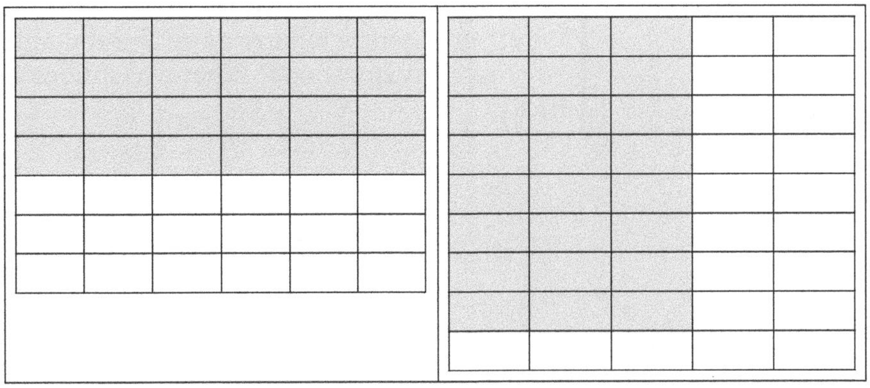 **Teacher:** I am going to give each one of you a problem. I want you to tell us what you did and explain your thinking.

Figure 5.10 Visual Student Activity

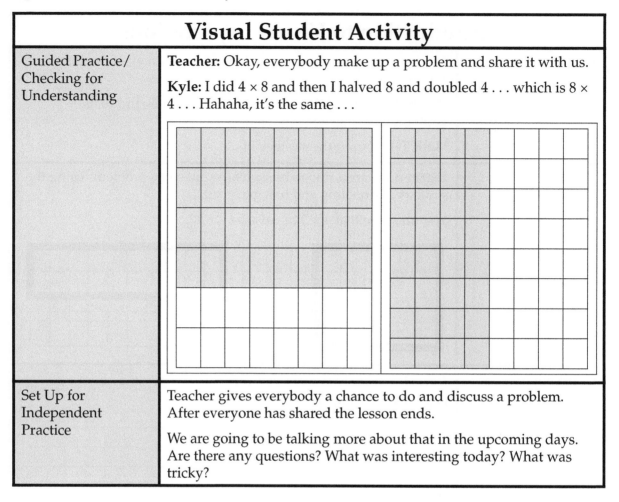

Guided Practice/ Checking for Understanding	**Teacher:** Okay, everybody make up a problem and share it with us. **Kyle:** I did 4 × 8 and then I halved 8 and doubled 4 . . . which is 8 × 4 . . . Hahaha, it's the same . . .
Set Up for Independent Practice	Teacher gives everybody a chance to do and discuss a problem. After everyone has shared the lesson ends. We are going to be talking more about that in the upcoming days. Are there any questions? What was interesting today? What was tricky?

Figure 5.11 Lesson Close

Close

♦ What did we do today?
♦ What was the math we were practicing?
♦ What were we doing with our sketches?
♦ Was this easy or tricky?
♦ Are there any questions?

Figure 5.12 Abstract Introduction

\multicolumn{2}{c}{**Introduction to Abstract Explorations**}	
Launch	**Teacher:** Today we are going to look at the strategy of doubling and halving. **Vocabulary:** Multiplication, multiplying, factors, products, doubling, halving, strategy, efficient **Math Talk:** I used the strategy of . . .
Model	**Teacher:** Today we are going to be looking at this strategy with larger numbers. For example 12 × 15. **Claire:** That's 6 × 30. That would be 180. **Teacher:** Let's look at 14 × 10. **Dan:** That's 7 × 20, which 140.
Checking for Understanding	**Teacher:** Okay, now, you I am going to give you a list of problems, and I want you to choose the ones that this strategy works best with. 4 x 5, 7 x 7, 10 x 5, 9 x 7, 5 x 5, 14 x 12 **Yoli:** I picked 4 × 5, and I did 2 × 10. **Danny:** I picked 10 × 5, and I got 5 × 10. **Marta:** I did 14 × 12; it can be 7 × 24.

Figure 5.13 Abstract Student Activity

Abstract Student Activity	
Guided Practice/ Checking for Understanding	**Teacher:** I want you to make up your own problems. **David:** I did 20 × 35, and that makes 10 × 70, which is 700. **Carol:** I did 15 × 12. That makes 30 × 6, which is 180.
Set Up for Independent Practice	The students come up with the answers and explain what they did. Teacher explains that this activity will be one of the choices in the workstations and that they should talk through different strategies with their math buddies.

Figure 5.14 Lesson Close

Close
◆ What did we do today?   ◆ What was the math we were practicing?   ◆ What were we doing with our multiplication expressions?   ◆ Was this easy or tricky?   ◆ Are there any questions?

Section Summary

Multidigit multiplication is the 5th-grade fluency. Many students have trouble doing it. It is important to teach the students many different strategies for thinking about multiplying 2-digit by 2-digit numbers. They have learned many of these strategies in 4th grade, hopefully. Although they should be focusing on the traditional algorithm in 5th grade, it is important to keep reinforcing different ways to think about numbers. Throughout the entire year, the teacher should do number talks and number string routines so that students become very comfortable talking about number relationships.

Figure 5.15 Overview

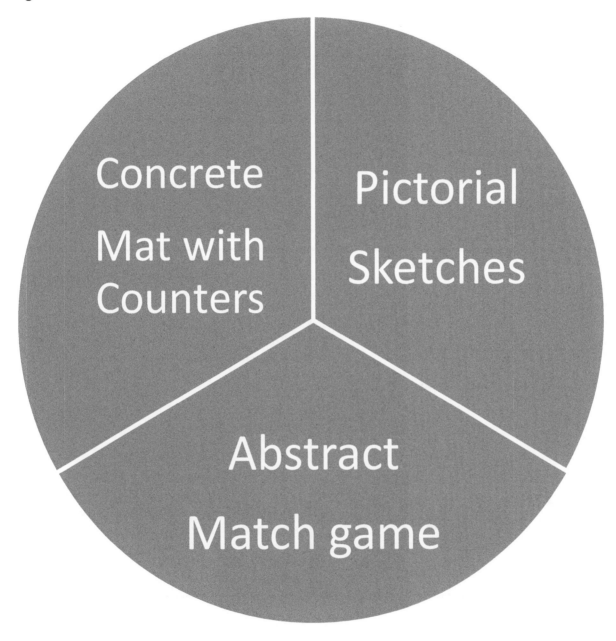

Figure 5.16 Planning Template

Division Mats

Big Idea: Numbers, Operation Meanings & Relationships; Properties, Basic Facts & Algorithms	**Materials** ♦ Tools: counters (tiles, cubes, circles)
Enduring Understanding: Students will understand that dividing can be sharing equally and that there can be leftovers/ remainders. **Essential Question:** Why is division important? How do we use it in real life? **I can statement:** I can model division problems with a remainder. I can explain and defend my thinking.	**Vocabulary & Language Frames** **Vocabulary:** factors, array, product, quotient, divisor, dividend **Math Talk:** The quotient is _____. There is a remainder of _____.

Cycle of Engagement	Math Processes/Practices
Concrete: $13 \div 4 = 3$ There is a remainder of 1. 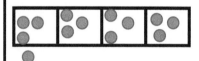 **Pictorial:** 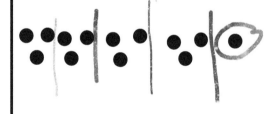	♦ Problem-Solving ♦ Reasoning ♦ Models ♦ Tools ♦ Precision ♦ Structure ♦ Pattern **Abstract:** $9 \div 4 = 2\ \frac{1}{2}$ *Students should do this problem in the context of a story so they can interpret the remainder. Writing the remainder with an R is mathematically incorrect.

Figure 5.17 Differentiation

3 Differentiated Lessons		
In this series of lessons, students are working on dividing and exploring remainders. They are developing this concept through concrete activities, pictorial activities and abstract activities. Here are some things to think about as you do these lessons.		
Emerging	**On Grade Level**	**Above Grade Level**
Division is more challenging than multiplication. Review subtraction. Also, do a great many problems using small numbers so students can visualize the math. Students should work on understanding concepts such as what happens when 0 is divided by a number, what happens when dividing by 1, 2, the number itself, etc. Although these are 3rd-grade concepts, many upper elementary students struggle with them through middle school.	The grade-level standard is that students can work with multidigit numbers for division. The focus should be on strategies. Remember that the traditional algorithm isn't a standard until 6th grade.	Have students come up with projects that explore when and how we use division in real life. They can do extended investigations and projects on something that interests them.

 Looking for Misunderstandings and Common Errors

Students have trouble with division. It is important to use division math mats with them because it helps them to physically act out the story as it is being told. After they do that, then they can do sketches. After they do that, they can move on to tape/bar diagrams. In 4th grade, students are supposed to learn about remainders. In 5th grade, be sure to review working with remainders from the beginning of the year before you take it to the next level because many students are still shaky on the concept. Have the students solve open problems using remainders too.

Figure 5.18 Anchor Chart

Modeling Division
325 ÷ 3

Concrete (Place Value Disks)

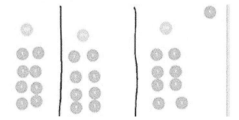

Pictorial (Tape Diagram)

$300 \div 3 = 100$

$24 \div 3 = 8$

remainder 1

100	+	8

300	24

$108\frac{1}{3}$

Abstract: $325 \div 3 = 108\frac{1}{3}$

Figure 5.19 Concrete Introduction

	Introduction to Concrete Explorations
Launch	**Teacher:** Today we are going to work on division. **Vocabulary:** Dividend, divisor, quotient, expression, equation **Math Talk:** The quotient is _____. The dividend is ____. The divisor is ____.
Model	**Teacher:** We are going to be telling division stories. We will use the division mats to help us with our thinking. Let's do it and then someone will explain their thinking to the group. Here is the first problem: *The answer is 4 with a remainder of 1.* Tell me a story about this problem. Work with a partner, and then we will come back and discuss together. ***Although this is a 4th-grade standard, this is a tricky activity for 5th graders because of the reasoning that students have to do.** **Kay & Dante:** So we thought about problems that have an answer of 4 first. So 16 divided by 4, or 20 divided by 5. Then we added a bit more so we would have a remainder. Then we made up a story. There are 4 kids. There were 17 marbles. How many marbles did each kid get if they got the same amount. Are there any left over?

Figure 5.19 (Continued)

Checking for Understanding	**Katie:** They each got 4 marbles with 1 left over. **Teacher:** Who wants to go next? Tell us a problem with a remainder. **Ray-Ray & Marta:** We did a measurement problem. We said the kids were going to make jump ropes. There were 4 kids that had 29 feet of rope. They were going to make jump ropes that were 7 feet long each. How much did each person get? How much rope was left over?     **Teacher:** Okay. I am going to give each one of you your own problem. I want you to read it. Solve it. Be ready to share how you did it. I am going to watch you, and if you need help, look at our anchor charts, ask a math partner and, of course, you can ask me.

Figure 5.20 Concrete Student Activity

Concrete Student Activity	
Guided Practice/ Checking for Understanding	The teacher gives the students a few more problems. As they do their work, the teacher takes notes, asks questions and has a conversation with individual students. **Teacher:** The next problem is $302 divided by 2 people. How much does each person get? **Donnie:** Well, we gave each person 100 and then 1 and then we split the other hundred into 10s and gave each person $50. So it 100 + 50 + 1 = 151. 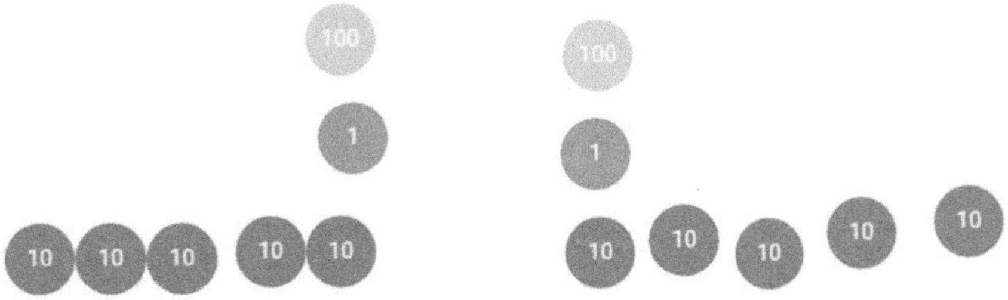
Set Up for Independent Practice	Every child shares out their problem and how they solved it their problem. **Teacher:** We are going to be talking more about this in the upcoming days. Are there any questions? What was interesting today? What was tricky?

Figure 5.21 Lesson Close

Close
◆ What did we do today? ◆ What was the math we were practicing? ◆ What were we doing with our division mats? ◆ Was this easy or tricky? ◆ Are there any questions?

Figure 5.22 Division Mat Example Cards

Problem	

leftover

Equation:

There is a remainder of _____.

Problem:				

leftover

Equation:

There is a remainder of _____.

Figure 5.23 Visual Introduction

Introduction to a Visual Explorations

Launch	**Teacher:** Today we are going to continue to work on division with remainders. **Vocabulary:** Dividend, divisor, quotient, expression, equation **Math Talk:** The quotient is _____. The dividend is _____. The divisor is _____.
Model	**Teacher:** Today we are going do what we did yesterday, but today we are doing math sketches to solve our problems. Who wants to share their thinking first? Here is a problem. Four kids shared $169. How much did each child get? **Tommy:** I did it. I gave everybody $25. That's the $100 shared. Then, I gave everybody $10. That's $40. I have $29 left. That means everybody gets $7 more and there is a $1 left. We could give each kid a quarter.  <table><tr><td colspan="4">There are 4 kids.</td></tr><tr><td>$25 $10 $7</td><td>$25 $10 $7</td><td>$25 $10 $7</td><td>$25 $10 $7</td></tr><tr><td colspan="4">1 leftover $1</td></tr></table>
Checking for Understanding	**Teacher:** Okay. I am going to give each one of you your own problem. I want you to read it. Solve it. Be ready to share how you did it. I am going to watch you and if you need help, look at our anchor charts, ask a math partner and, of course, you can ask me.

Figure 5.24 Visual Student Activity

	Visual Student Activity
Guided Practice/ Checking for Understanding	**Teacher:** Next problem. There are 14 kids, and they have to share $200. How much does each kid get? **Kimi:** Well you could split up the $140 first. That means each kid gets $10. Then you have $60 left. So, I am thinking multiplication. Each child could get $4. I could draw it like this. 10 + 4 | $200 -$140 $ 60	$60 -$ 56 4 | $4 left
Set Up for Independent Practice	Every child shares out their problem and how they solved it. **Teacher:** We are going to be talking more about this in the upcoming days. Are there any questions? What was interesting today? What was tricky?

Figure 5.25 Lesson Close

Close
♦ What did we do today? ♦ What was the math we were practicing? ♦ What were we doing with our math sketches? ♦ Was this easy or tricky? ♦ Are there any questions?

Figure 5.26 More Examples of Division Mats

leftover

Equation:

There is a remainder of _____.

Write a division problem with a remainder.

Solve:

Figure 5.27 Abstract Introduction

Introduction to Abstract Explorations	
Launch	**Teacher:** Today we are going to continue to work on division. **Vocabulary:** Dividend, divisor, quotient, expression, equation **Math Talk:** The quotient is _____. The dividend is _____. The divisor is _____.
Model	**Teacher:** There are many different things that you can do when you have a remainder. Today we are going to tell stories where we think and talk about that. For example, if I tell you the problem is $105 \div 10 = 10$ There is a remainder of 5. Tell me a story where you have to round up because of the remainder. Let's talk about pencils. **Mikela:** The store has 105 pencils. They are going to put 10 in a bag. How many bags will they need? They will need 11 because they need a bag for the leftover 5 pencils. Or they could give those 5 away as gifts.
Checking for Understanding	**Teacher:** Okay, next story. Tell me a story with a remainder between 2 and 5. **Mimi:** 15 kids shared $152. They each got $10, and there were $2 leftover.

Figure 5.28 Abstract Student Activity

Abstract Student Activity	
Guided Practice/ Checking for Understanding	**Teacher:** Okay, next story. Tell me a division story with a 2-digit divisor and a remainder between 5 and 7. **Mark:** The toy store packed marbles. They had 15 boxes and 155 marbles. How many marbles did they put in each box? **Yesenia:** Well, 10×15 is 150 so . . . they put 10 in a box, and there were 5 marbles left over.
Set Up for Independent Practice	**Teacher:** So, when we have a remainder there are lots of different things that can happen to it depending on what the problem is asking. Who can tell me more about that? **Tami:** Sometimes you drop it. **Mike:** Sometimes you have to include it. **Teddy:** Sometimes you can share it . . . like the problem we did on the rug. After all the students share, the teacher wraps up the lesson, and the students go to their workstations.

Figure 5.29 Lesson Close

Close
◆ What did we do today? ◆ What was the math we were practicing? ◆ What were we doing with our remainder stories? ◆ Was this easy or tricky? ◆ Are there any questions?

Section Summary

Division is tricky for students. They must have plenty of opportunities where they get to act out word problems. The problems should be real-life contexts so that students can understand what they are talking about. They should act out the problem with manipulatives, then sketch out the problems and, finally, be able to solve the problems with symbols. Students should be able to talk about the relationships between concrete, pictorial and abstract representations of the same problem.

Multiplying Double-Digit Numbers

Figure 5.30 Overview

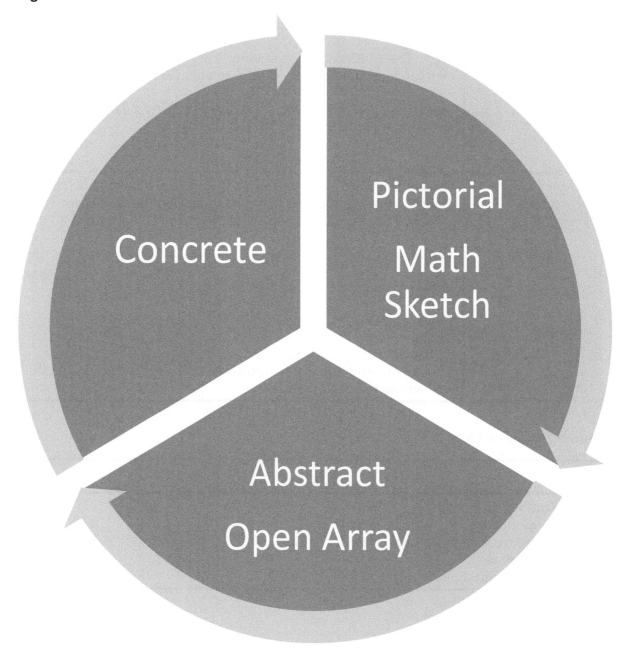

Figure 5.31 Planning Template

Multiplying 2-Digit Numbers

Big Idea: Numbers, Operation Meanings & Relationships; Properties, Basic Facts & Algorithms **Enduring Understanding:** Students will understand different ways to model and represent multiplying 2-digit numbers by 2-digit numbers. **Essential Question:** Why is 2-digit multiplication important? How do we use it in real life? **I can statement:** I can use different strategies to model multiplication of 2-digit number by 2-digit numbers.	**Materials** ♦ Tools: counters (tiles, cubes, circles)
	Vocabulary & Language Frames **Vocabulary:** multiply, multiplication, addition, sum, factor, product, strategy, partial products **Math Talk:** My strategy was _____. My model was _____.

Cycle of Engagement	**Abstract:**	**Math Processes/ Practices**
Concrete: **Pictorial:**	$12 \times 13 = 156$ $10 \times 10 = 100$ $10 \times 3 = 30$ $2 \times 10 = 20$ $2 \times 3 = 6$	♦ Problem-Solving ♦ Reasoning ♦ Models ♦ Tools ♦ Precision ♦ Structure ♦ Pattern

Figure 5.32 Differentiation

3 Differentiated Lessons
In this series of lessons, students are working on double-digit multiplication. Students should be developing this concept through concrete activities, pictorial activities and abstract activities. Here are some things to think about as you do these lessons.

Emerging	On Grade Level	Above Grade Level
Do a lot of work with manipulatives. Make sure students know their facts within 100. Also make sure they are comfortable with their 11s and 12s. They have started working with this in 4th grade, but now in 5th grade, it is about fluency.	Do a lot of work with different manipulatives and have the students do area models and open arrays as stated in the standards. Also continue to work with various strategies. The fluency is that students can do 2-digit by 2-digit.	Students can do different projects on multiplication in real life. They should come up with different topics that they want to explore about the ways in which multiplication is used in our day-to-day living.

 Looking for Misunderstandings and Common Errors

Students have trouble with 2-digit multiplication because the place values get bigger and the number of steps and numbers get larger. This means there is more opportunity for mistakes in adding all the little parts. Start with the concrete and visual models that allow students to look at partial products. Students should understand how to estimate a product and understand if their answer is reasonable. Be sure to do worked examples with students in which you show them some of their common errors and ask them to find them and discuss them. Students will regroup incorrectly, they will misalign the numbers in the traditional algorithm and sometimes they will simply multiply incorrectly. Scaffold the work as well. See if students can multiply single-digit numbers, then a single digit by a double digit, then a triple digit, then a double-digit by a double-digit and then a double digit by a triple digit. It is important to see where the error patterns are and exactly what they are.

Figure 5.33 Anchor Chart

Modeling Double-digit multiplication

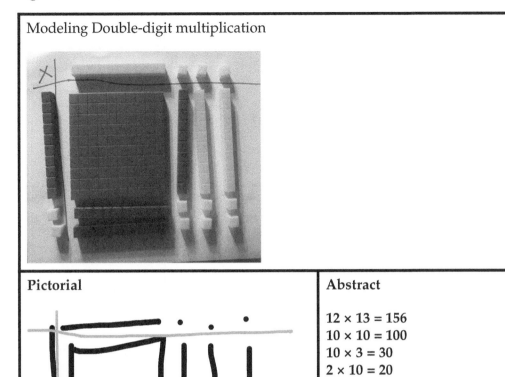

Pictorial	Abstract
	$12 \times 13 = 156$ $10 \times 10 = 100$ $10 \times 3 = 30$ $2 \times 10 = 20$ $2 \times 3 = 6$

Figure 5.34 Concrete Introduction

	Introduction to Concrete Explorations
Launch	**Teacher:** Today we are going to work on multiplying 2-digit numbers by 2-digit numbers. **Vocabulary:** multiply, multiplication, addition, sum, factor, product, strategy, partial products **Math Talk:** My strategy was . . .
Model	**Teacher:** Today we are going to explore with base 10 blocks. Let's explore 12×13. **Tyler:** I did 10×10 which is 100. 10×3, which is 30. 2×10, which is 20. 2×3, which is 6. That makes 156.
Checking for Understanding	**Teacher:** Let's do another one. Turn and tell your partner what you did, and then someone will explain their thinking out to the group. 12×11 **Kimi:** I did $10 \times 10 = 100$ $10 \times 1 = 10$ $2 \times 10 = 20$ $2 \times 1 = 2$ That makes 132. **Teacher:** Okay. I am going to give each one of you your own problem. Solve it. Be ready to share how you did it. I am going to watch you, and if you need help, look at our anchor charts, ask a math partner and, of course, you can ask me.

Figure 5.35 Concrete Student Activity

	Concrete Student Activity
Guided Practice/ Checking for Understanding	**Teacher**: Let's look at another problem. Jamal, explain what you did. 12 x 12 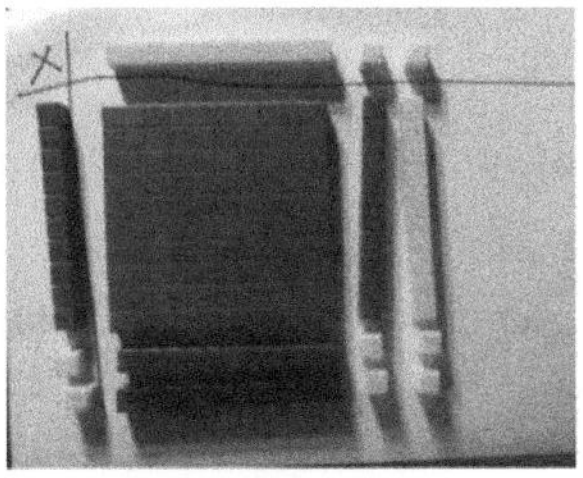 **Jamal:** $10 \times 10 = 100$ $10 \times 2 = 20$ $2 \times 10 = 20$ $2 \times 2 = 4$ Answer is 144.
Set Up for Independent Practice	Every child shares their problem and how they solved it. We are going to be talking more about that in the upcoming days. Are there any questions? What was interesting today? What was tricky?

Figure 5.36 Lesson Close

Close
♦ What did we do today? ♦ What was the math we were practicing? ♦ What were we doing with our base 10 blocks? ♦ Was this easy or tricky? ♦ Are there any questions?

Figure 5.37 Problem Template

Problem:

Explain your work

Figure 5.38 Visual Introduction

Introduction to a Visual Explorations

Launch	**Teacher:** Today we are going to work on multiplying 2-digit numbers by 2-digit numbers. **Vocabulary:** multiply, multiplication, addition, sum, factor, product, strategy, partial products **Math Talk:** My strategy was . . .
Model	**Teacher:** I want you all to make up your own problem and model it with a base ten sketch. Okay, who wants to go first? **Hong:** I did 12 × 12. I got 144. 
Checking for Understanding	**Teacher: Who wants to go next?** **Daniel:** I did 12 × 11 and I got 132. 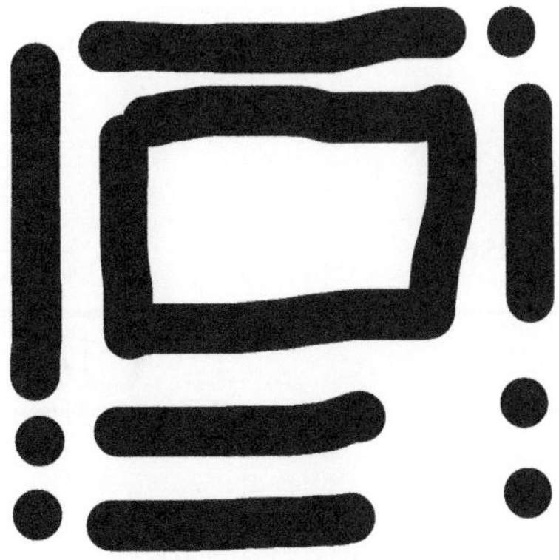 **Teacher:** Okay. I am going to give each one of you your own problem. I want you to solve it. Model it with a sketch and then be ready to share how you did it. I am going to watch you, and if you need help, look at our anchor charts, ask a math partner and, of course, you can ask me.

Figure 5.39 Visual Student Activity

Visual Student Activity	
Guided Practice/ Checking for Understanding	**Teacher:** Kay, explain your problem to us. **Kay:** I did 14 × 13, and I got 182. 
Set Up for Independent Practice	Teacher gives everybody a chance to do and discuss a problem. After everyone has shared, the lesson ends. **Teacher:** We are going to be talking more about this in the upcoming days. Are there any questions? What was interesting today? What was tricky?

Figure 5.40 Lesson Close

Close
◆ What did we do today? ◆ What was the math we were practicing? ◆ What were we doing with our sketches? ◆ Was this easy or tricky? ◆ Are there any questions?

Figure 5.41 Drawing Equations

Equation	Drawing

Figure 5.42 Abstract Introduction

Introduction to Abstract Explorations	
Launch	**Teacher:** Today we are going to work on multiplying 2-digit numbers by 2-digit numbers. **Vocabulary:** multiply, multiplication, addition, sum, factor, product, strategy, partial products **Math Talk: My strategy was . . .**
Model	**Teacher:** We have been working on various strategies. I want you to write a problem and solve it using a strategy. **Katie:** I did 15 × 4, and then I did 30 × 2, which is 60. I did doubling and halving. **Trina:** I did 12 × 10, and I got 6 × 20, which is 120. I did doubling and halving too.
Checking for Understanding	**Teacher:** Okay, who wants to go next. I want you to also think about some other strategies. **Grace:** I did 22 × 15, and so I did: 20 × 10, which is 200. 20 × 5, which is 100. 2 × 10, which is 20. 2 × 5, which is 10. I got 330 **Kim:** I did 15 × 15, and so I did 15 × 10, which is 150, and then 15 × 5, which is 75, and that makes 225.

Figure 5.43 Abstract Student Activity

	Abstract Student Activity
Guided Practice/ Checking for Understanding	**Teacher:** Who wants to go next? **Misha:** I did 12 × 12. I did 10 × 12, which is 120, and then 2 × 12, which is 24, and I added those together and I got 144.
Set Up for Independent Practice	The teacher continues to ask the students questions about their strategies. The teacher is taking notes as the students discuss their thinking.

Section Summary

It is important to give students a chance to try out different strategies and models and discuss them. Students should have the opportunity to make up their own problems as well as be given problem sets by the teacher. Students should use at least the models of open array and area models. They should also use equations (with various strategies). Students will often get comfortable with one strategy and always use that strategy, so it is important to have them solve one way and check another.

Division of a 3-Digit Number Divided by a 2-Digit Number

Figure 5.44 Overview

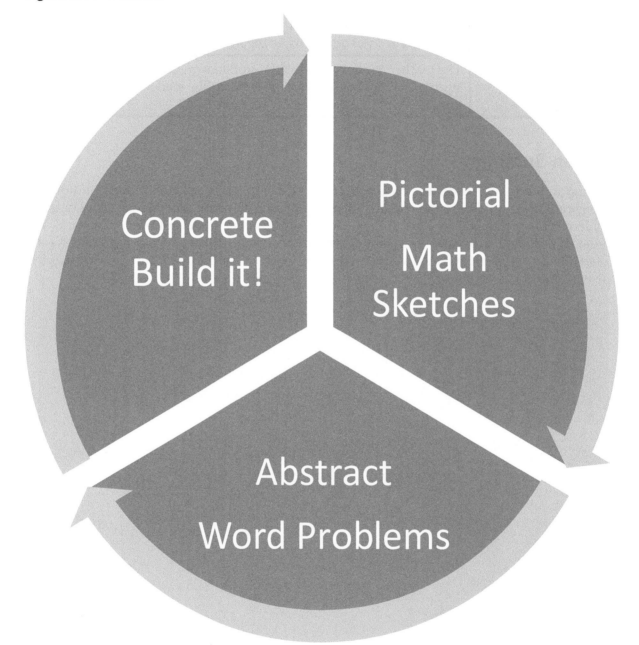

Figure 5.45 Planning Template

Division of Three-Digit Numbers	
Big Idea: Numbers, Operation Meanings & Relationships; Properties, Basic Facts & Algorithms **Enduring Understanding:** Students will understand different ways to model and represent division of multidigit numbers. **Essential Question:** Why is division important? How do we use it in real life? **I can statement:** I can show different ways to model division of multidigit numbers.	**Materials** ♦ Tools: counters (tiles, cubes, circles)
	Vocabulary & Language Frames **Vocabulary:** divisor, dividend, quotient, partial quotients, model, strategy **Math Talk:** The quotient is _____. The remainder is _____.
Cycle of Engagement **Concrete:** 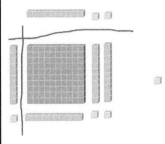 **Pictorial:**  **Abstract:** 133 ÷ 11 = 12 There is a remainder of 1.	**Math Processes/Practices** ♦ Problem-Solving ♦ Reasoning ♦ Models ♦ Tools ♦ Precision ♦ Structure ♦ Pattern

Figure 5.46 Differentiation

3 Differentiated Lessons		
In this series of lessons, students are working on dividing three-digit numbers by two-digit numbers. They are developing this concept through concrete activities, pictorial activities and abstract activities. Here are some things to think about as you do these lessons.		
Emerging	**On Grade Level**	**Above Grade Level**
Do a lot of work with manipulatives. Review basic division within 100 (3rd grade). Also review dividing double- and triple-digit numbers by a single digit (4th grade).	Do a lot of work with different manipulatives and have the students do math sketches and diagrams. Make sure to scaffold the concept by first focusing intensely on 2-digit numbers and then connect this to more multi-digit numbers so that you are accelerating the instruction and students are working on grade level standards.	Have students develop a project about division in real life and work on it throughout the unit.

 Looking for Misunderstandings and Common Errors

Students have trouble with division in general. Start with small numbers and problems that they can visualize before going on to larger numbers. Grossnickle (1936) found that there are 57 errors in long division, although many are infrequent. There are some errors that are very common. Students have trouble regrouping. They have trouble with their multiplication facts. They have a great deal of trouble with zeros in any place. They have trouble with subtraction. They also have a great deal of trouble interpreting remainders.

Figure 5.47 Anchor Chart

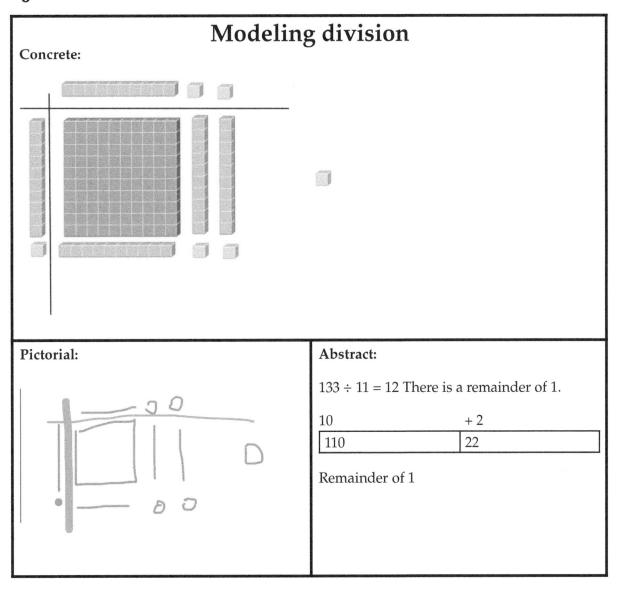

Modeling division

Concrete:

Pictorial:

Abstract:

$133 \div 11 = 12$ There is a remainder of 1.

10	+ 2
110	22

Remainder of 1

Figure 5.48 Concrete Introduction

Introduction to Concrete Explorations

Launch	**Teacher:** Today we are going to work on remainder stories. **Vocabulary:** dividend, divisor, quotient, expression, equation **Math Talk:** The quotient is _____. The dividend is _____. The divisor is _____.
Model	**Teacher:** Let's all take our mats. Count out 144 and divide it by 12. What do you notice? **Ivan:** I see that it is a rectangle. The quotient is 12. 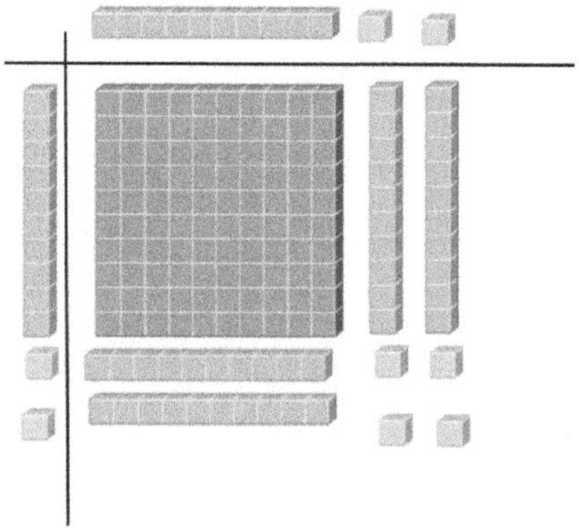
Checking for Understanding	**Teacher:** Okay, here is another problem: 156 divided by 15. Who wants to explain what they did? **Johnny:** I do. I know that because 10 × 15 is 150, so I built that, and then I had 6 leftover. 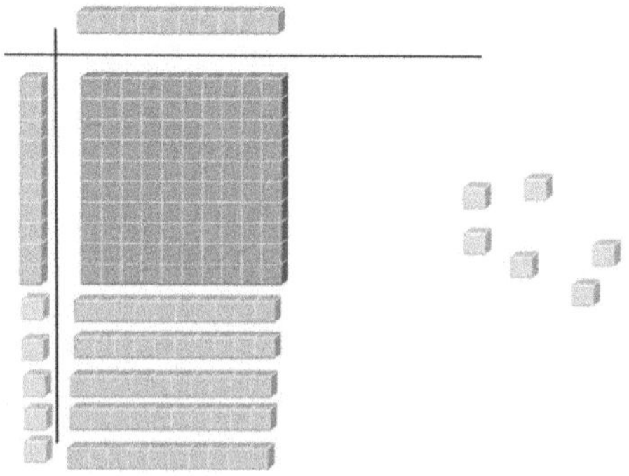 **Teacher:** Okay. I am going to give each one of you your own problem. I want you to read it. Solve it. Be ready to share how you did it. I am going to watch you and if you need help, look at our anchor charts and, of course, you can ask me.

Figure 5.49 Concrete Student Activity

	Concrete Student Activity
Guided Practice/ Checking for Understanding	Students act out various problems and the teacher watches, takes notes and asks the students questions. **Teacher:** Marcos, tell me how you solved that problem. **Marcos:** I thought about multiplication. I know that 12 × 12 is 144, so then 147 would mean that there are 3 left over. Here is how I modeled that. 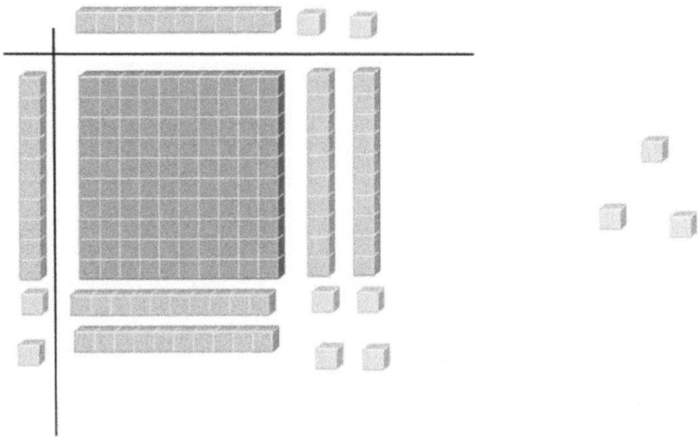
Set Up for Independent Practice	Teacher gives everybody a chance to do and discuss a problem. After everyone has shared, the lesson ends. **Teacher:** We are going to be talking more about this in the upcoming days. Are there any questions? What was interesting today? What was tricky?

Figure 5.50 Lesson Close

Close
◆ What did we do today? ◆ What was the math we were practicing? ◆ What were we doing with our division mats? ◆ Was this easy or tricky? ◆ Are there any questions?

Figure 5.51 Division Mat

Problem:

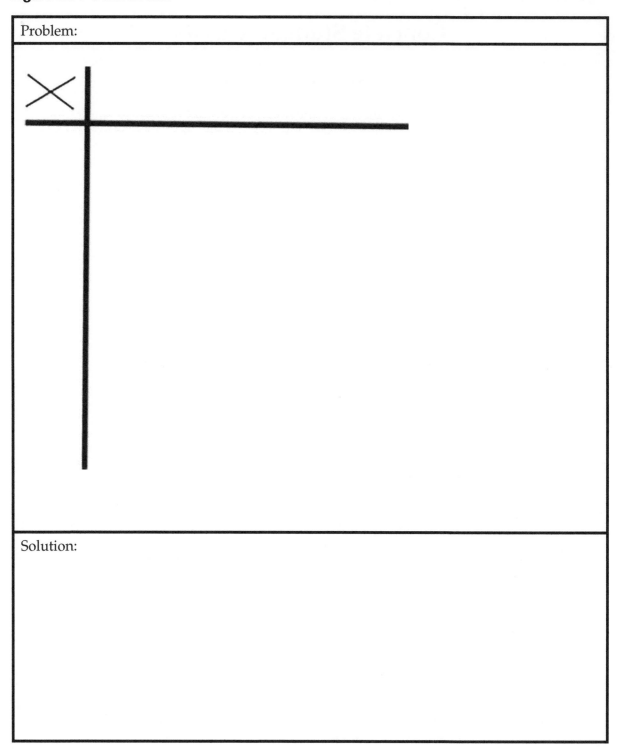

Solution:

Figure 5.52 Visual Introduction

Introduction to a Visual Explorations

Launch	**Teacher:** Today we are going to work on dividing multi=digit numbers and tape diagrams. **Vocabulary:** dividend, divisor, quotient, expression, equation **Math Talk:** The quotient is _____. The dividend is _____. The divisor is _____.
Model	**Teacher:** Today we are going to model division with math sketches. I want you to solve this problem, and then somebody share their thinking: I had 267 divided by 13. **Mariana:** I thought multiplication and I know that 13 × 10 is 130. I did it twice, and then I had 7 left over. I used an array model. 10 + 10 | 130 | 130 | The remainder is 7
Checking for Understanding	Students do 2 more problems together, and then the teacher lets them work on their own.

Figure 5.53 Student Visual activity

Pictorial Student Activity

Guided Practice/ Checking for Understanding	**Teacher:** Hong, tell me how you solved that problem. **Hong:** I had 250 divided by 12. I did 120 and then 120 again; that was 240 and 10 more left over. 10 + 10 | 120 | 120 | **The remainder is 10.**
Set Up for Independent Practice	Teacher gives everybody a chance to do and discuss a problem. After everyone has shared the lesson ends. We are going to be talking more about this in the upcoming days. Are there any questions? What was interesting today? What was tricky?

Figure 5.54 Lesson Close

Close
♦ What did we do today?   ♦ What was the math we were practicing?   ♦ What were we doing with our sketches?   ♦ Was this easy or tricky?   ♦ Are there any questions?

Figure 5.55 Division Mat Example

Model it!
Work area (explain your thinking)   Leftovers/Remainders

Figure 5.56 Abstract Introduction

	Introduction to Abstract Explorations
Launch	**Teacher:** Today we are going to work on division. **Vocabulary:** dividend, divisor, quotient, expression, equation **Math Talk:** The quotient is _____. The dividend is _____. The divisor is _____.
Model	**Teacher:** Today we are going to talk more about strategies. If I had 240 divided by 16, what could I do? **Todd:** We were talking about this on the rug. If the numbers are friendly, then you could halve and halve. So we could try 120 divided by 8. We could break it apart and divide 80 by 8, and so that's 10, and then we have 40 left, and that divided by 8 is 5. So together 10 and 5 would by 15. Let me check. . . . Yep, that works because 15×16 is 240.
Checking for Understanding	**Teacher:** Let's look at another one 389 divided by 17. **Jada:** I'm going to think multiplication . . . so 17×20 is 340, and that is 49 left. So divided by 17 is 2, and there is a remainder of 15? Let me see:

<table>
<tr><td>20</td><td>+</td><td>2</td></tr>
<tr><td>389
-340
  49</td><td></td><td>49
-34
15</td></tr>
</table>

Teacher: So today we are looking at how you can break apart a dividend to make it easier to divide. You can then divide it in parts and then put those parts back together.

Figure 5.57 Abstract Student Activity

Abstract Student Activity	
Guided Practice/ Checking for Understanding	**Teacher:** Okay, let's do another problem: 444 ÷ 12. **John:** I'll explain. I'm going to use an open array. So I took out 360 because I know that is a multiple of 12, and then there is 84 left. Then 84 divided by 12 is 7. So 30 + 7 is 37. 30 + 7 444 84 -360 -84 84 0
Set Up for Independent Practice	The teacher continues to ask the students questions about their strategies as they work on problems. After they finish, the students go to various workstations.

Figure 5.58 Lesson Close

Close
◆ What did we do today?   ◆ What was the math we were practicing?   ◆ What were we doing with our open arrays?   ◆ Was this easy or tricky?   ◆ Are there any questions?

Section Summary

Open arrays are part of the math standards in 4th grade, but many people do not teach them. In 5th grade, I always find that it is important to review dividing multidigit numbers by single-digit numbers before diving headfirst into multidigit numbers by double-digit numbers. As teachers, we all must get more comfortable doing them and coming up with strategies for breaking apart numbers. This can be tricky for teachers because most of us did not learn this way. So, we have to learn it so we can teach it to our students. It is really important to spend time working on breaking apart numbers that are divisible by the divisor. The idea of partial quotients is a powerful concept, and we need to spend a great deal more time than we usually do on it in schools. There are more and more great videos now on teaching with open arrays as well.

Depth of Knowledge

Depth of Knowledge (DoK) is a framework that encourages us to ask questions that require that students to think, reason, explain, defend and justify their thinking (Webb, 2002). Here is snapshot of what that can look like in terms of place-value work.

Figure 5.59 DoK Activities

	How can doubling and halving help us with multi-digit numbers.	What are different strategies and models that we can use to teach division with remainders?	What are different strategies and models to teach multiplication of a double-digit number by a double-digit number?	What are different strategies and models to teach division of multidigit numbers?
DoK Level 1 (These are questions that require students to simply recall/ reproduce an answer/do a procedure.)	Solve using the double and halve strategy. 12 × 15	Solve: 458 ÷ 15	Solve: 30 × 43	Solve: 377 ÷ 19
DoK Level 2 (These are questions that have students use information and think about concepts and reason.)	Solve: using the double and halve strategy: 12 × 8. Draw a model and explain your thinking. Then, discuss another way that you could do it.	Solve: 458 ÷ 15 Tell a story about this equation. Model and explain your thinking.	Solve: 30 × 43 in 2 different ways. Model and explain your thinking.	Solve: 377 ÷ 19 Estimate the quotient. Model and explain your thinking.
DoK Level 3 (These are questions that have students reason, plan, explain, justify and defend their thinking.)	Write and solve a word problem in which you double and halve the numbers.	Write and solve a word problem in which the remainder is in between 5 and 8.	Write and solve a multiplication word problem with an answer between 400–500.	Write and solve a word problem in which you divide a 3 or 4-digit number by a 2- or 3-digit number.

Adapted from Kaplinsky (https://robertkaplinsky.com/depth-knowledge-matrix-elementary-math/). A great resource for asking open questions is Marion Small's *Good Questions: Great Ways to Differentiate Mathematics Instruction in the Standards-Based Classroom* (2017).

Also Robert Kaplinsky has done a great job in pushing our thinking forward with the DoK matrices he created. The Kentucky Department of Education also has a great DoK math matrix (2007).

Figure 5.60 Asking Rigorous Questions

DoK 1	DoK 2 At this level, students explain their thinking.	DoK 3 At this level, students have to justify, defend and prove their thinking with objects, drawings and diagrams.
What is the answer to . . . Can you model the number? Can you model the problem? Can you identify the answer that matches this equation?	How do you know that the equation is correct? Can you pick the correct answer and explain why it is correct? How can you model that problem? What is another way to model that problem? Can you model that on the . . . Give me an example of a . . . type of problem. Which answer is incorrect? Explain your thinking?	Can you prove that your answer is correct? Prove that . . . Explain why that is the answer . . . Show me how to solve that and explain what you are doing. Defend your thinking.

Key Points

♦ Building Arrays
♦ Division
♦ Missing Numbers
♦ Distributive Property

Chapter Summary

Fluency is very important in 5th grade. It is much more than just knowing what the answer is to a problem. Students have to be able to contextualize problems. They should be able to tell stories about addition, subtraction, multiplication and division. They should have plenty of opportunities to work on missing numbers and make the connections between the operations. They should understand the properties. They should work with concrete manipulatives, do math sketches and work with symbols. This takes time across the year.

Reflection Questions

1. How are you currently doing fluency lessons? Are you engaging in distributed practice throughout the year?
2. Are you making sure that you do concrete, pictorial and abstract activities?
3. What do your students struggle with the most, and what ideas are you taking away from this chapter that might inform your work around those struggles?

References

Baroody, J., Purpura, D., Eiland, M., Reid, E., & Paliwal, V. (2016). Does Fostering Reasoning Strateigeis for Relatively Difficult Combinations Promote Transfer by K-3 Students? *Journal of Educational Psychology*, 108(4).

Brownell, W. A. (1956, October). Meaning and Skill-Maintaining the Balance. *Arithmetic Teacher*, 3, 129–136.

Brownell, W. A., & Chazal, C. B. (1935, September). The Effects of Premature Drill in Third-Grade Arithmetic. *Journal of Educational Research*, 29, 17–28.

Boaler, J. (2015). Fluency Without Fear: Research Evidence on the Best Ways to Learn Math Facts. Retrieved on September 6, 2019, from www.youcubed.org/evidence/fluency-without-fear/.

Godfrey, C., & Stone, J. (2013). Mastering Fact Fluency: Are They Game? *Teaching Children Mathematics*, V20(2), 96–101.

Grossnickle, F. E. (1936). Transfer of Knowledge of Multiplication Facts to Their Use in Long Division. *The Journal of Educational Research*, 29(9), 677–685. DOI: 10.1080/00220671.1936.10880633.

Henry, V., & Brown, R. (2008). First-Grade Basic Facts: An Investigation into Teaching and Learning of an Accelerated, High-Demand Memorization Standard. *Journal for Research in Mathematics Education*, 39(2), 153–183.

Kentucky Department of Education. (2007). Support Materials for Core Content for Assessment Version 4.1 Mathematics. Retrieved on January 15, 2017, from the internet.

Kilpatrick, J., Swafford, J., Findell, B., & National Research Council (U.S.). (2001). *Adding It Up: Helping Children Learn Mathematics*. Washington, DC: National Academy Press.

Mathematics Learning Study Committee, Center for Education, Division of Behavioral and Social Sciences and Education, National Research Council; Kilpatrick, J., Swafford, J., and Findell, B. (Eds.). (2001). *Adding It Up: Helping Children Learn Mathematics*. Washington, DC: National Academy Press.

National Center for Education Evaluation and Regional Assistance. (2009). Assisting Students Struggling with Mathematics: Response to Intervention (RtI) for Elementary and Middle Schools. 2009–4060. IES Retrieved from http://ies.ed.gov/ncee and http://ies. ed.gov/ncee/wwc/publications/practiceguides/.

National Council of Teachers of Mathematics. (2000). *Principles and Standards for School Mathematics*. Reston, VA: National Council of Teachers of Mathematics.

Newton, R. (2016). *Math Running Records*. New York: Routledge.

Newton, R., Record, A., & Mello, A. (2020). *Fluency Doesn't Just Happen.* New York: Routledge.

Smalls, M. (2017). *Good Questions: Great Ways to Differentiate Mathematics Instructions* (3rd edition). New York: TC Press.

Thornton, C. (1978). Emphasizing Thinking Strategies in Basic Fact Instruction. *Journal for Research in Mathematics Education,* V9(3), 214–227. NCTM. Reston, VA.

Van de Walle, J. A. (2007). *Elementary and Middle School Mathematics: Teaching Developmentally.* Boston: Pearson/Allyn and Bacon.

Webb, N. (2002). An Analysis of the Alignment between Mathematics Standards and Assessments for Three States. Paper Presented at the Annual Meeting of the American Educational Research Association, New Orleans, LA.

6

Small-Group Word Problem Lessons

It is important to teach about word problems in small guided math groups. Word problems have a specific learning trajectory as outlined in *the Cognitively Guided Instruction* work (Carpenter, Fennema, Franke, Levi, & Empson, 1999, 2015). There are specific categories and types of problems. Students should get an opportunity to explore solving various problems in various ways. This work should be scaffolded in the guided math group.

Every state has outlined the types of problems by grades that students should be working on. In the guided math group, teachers scaffold the learning so that students are working in their zone of proximal development toward the grade-level standards. The reality is that some problems are more challenging than others. Also, even within categories, number ranges can vary and should be scaffolded.

In this chapter, we look at various problems, including a few traditional problems about time and measurement. We explore 3-read protocol problems in which students have to make the questions and then solve them. We also look at open problems where there is context, and then students make up the entire problem and solve it with a model. We also look at picture word problem prompts that students have to make up the story for.

Research Note 🔍

♦ Students have a tendency to "suspend sense-making" when they are solving problems. They don't stop to reason through the problem (Schoenfeld, 1991; Verschaffel, Greer, & De Corte, 2000). We must find ways to slow the process down so they can think.

♦ Students develop a "compulsion to calculate" (Stacey & MacGregor, 1999) that can interfere with the development of the algebraic thinking that is needed to solve word problems (cited in www.cde.state.co.us/comath/word-problems-guide).

♦ Research consistently states that we should **never use key words**. From the beginning, teach students to reason about the context, not to depend on key words. See a great blog post that cites many articles on this: https://gfletchy.com/2015/01/12/teaching-key-words-forget-about-it/.

In this chapter we explore:

♦ Measurement Problems
♦ Decimal Problems
♦ Fraction Problems
♦ 3-Read Problems
♦ Picture Prompts
♦ Open Word Problems

DOI: 10.4324/9781003169666-6

Measurement Problems Overview

Figure 6.1 Overview

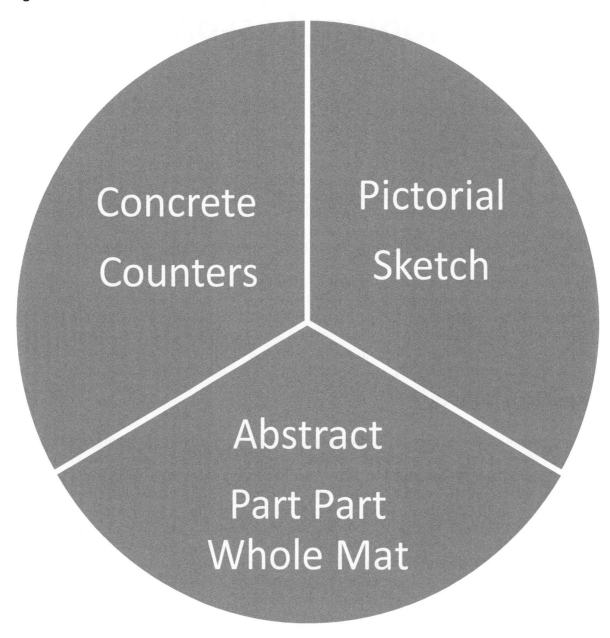

Figure 6.2 Planning Template

Measurement Word Problems	
Big Idea: Numbers, Operation Meanings & Relationships **Enduring Understanding:** Students understand that there are many different ways to model problems. **Essential Question:** What are the ways to model measurement problems? **I can statement:** I can model measurement problems. I can use different strategies to solve measurement problems.	**Materials** ♦ Tools: Measurement Cups ♦ Templates: Measurement Cups ♦ Cards ♦ Crayons
Cycle of Engagement **Concrete:**  **Pictorial: Drawing** 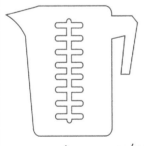 www.vecteezy.com/measuring cup **Abstract:** Sue poured some milk into the cake mix. Then, she poured 500 ml more. Now she has 1.25 liters. How much did she start with?	Vocabulary & Language Frames ♦ Beakers ♦ Measurement Cups ♦ Start ♦ Change ♦ End ♦ Liters ♦ Milliliters **My strategy was _____.** **My model was _____.**

Figure 6.3 Differentiation

3 Differentiated Lessons

In this series of lessons, students are working on the concept of *measurement problems*. They are developing this concept through concrete activities, pictorial activities and abstract activities. Everybody should do the cycle. Some students progress through it more quickly than others. Here are some things to think about as you do these lessons.

Emergent	On Grade Level	Above Grade Level
Review measurements. As you introduce this to students, do a lot of work by acting it out and then doing it with manipulatives. Be sure to have students draw what they acted out and connect it to number models.	The grade-level standard is that students can do conversions within a system. Students also are working with decimals. So do lots of this work where students are modeling it and explaining it.	Extend the number range.

 Looking for Misunderstandings and Common Errors

Measurement is a very tricky topic for students. Students need to have hands-on experiences with it. Things like Peter Liter and Gallon Man can be abstract visuals, but students need concrete experiences with different types of measurement. They should act out the problems at the small-group table amid conversation and discussion about the topic.

Figure 6.4 Concrete Introduction

	Introduction of Concrete Explorations: Open Measurement Problems
Launch	**Teacher:** Today we are going to do a measurement activity (make sure you send home letters about any allergies before you do this and get them signed by parents for participation). **Vocabulary:** cups, pints, quarts, capacity, measure **Math talk:** We used _____ ml. My model was . . . My strategy was . . .
Model	Today we are going to talk about making fruit punch. Grandma has 3 ingredients. She has some orange juice, some pineapple juice and some cranberry juice. She wants to make a pint of punch. What could some possibilities for the recipe be? Students taste test and work together to come up with a recipe for what the punch could be. They talk about what they like, what they don't like and what the strong flavor should be. They then try out the recipe at the table with the teacher asking questions. <table><tr><td colspan="2" align="center">Record of Thinking</td></tr><tr><td>1st Try</td><td>2nd Try</td></tr><tr><td> </td><td></td></tr></table>
Checking for Understanding	**Teacher:** Who can tell me about one of your recipes? **Maite:** We tried 4 ounces of apple juice, 1 cup of orange juice and 4 ounces of pineapple juice. **Ted:** We liked it!

Figure 6.5 Concrete Student Activity

Concrete Student Activity	
Guided Practice/ Checking for Understanding	The teacher watches the students try different recipes and then asks them about conversions. **Teacher:** Taylor, tell me about what your group is doing? **Taylor:** We are making a pint. We are trying different measurements. We know that there are 2 cups in a pint. We also know that there are 8 ounces in a cup. So we can play around. **Mike:** We did 1/2 a cup of apple, orange juice, mango and pineapple juice, and we didn't like it. **Marta:** We also tried a cup of orange juice and a cup of mango, and we loved it!
Set Up for Independent Practice	**Teacher:** That is great! We are going to continue working with the measuring cups at the workstations and do some drawings.

Figure 6.6 Lesson Close

Close
◆ What did we do today? ◆ What was the math we were practicing? ◆ What were we doing with the measuring cups and spoons? ◆ Was this easy or tricky? ◆ Are there any questions?

Figure 6.7 Problem Cards

Mike drank a pint of water during the day. What are the different amounts that he could have drank throughout the day?	Carla drank 2 pints of milk in the morning and then some more in the afternoon. Altogether, she drank a quart. How much did she drink in the afternoon?
Ricky drank 2 cups of water in the morning and 1 cup of water in the afternoon. He drank some more in the evening. He drank a total of a quart of water. How much did he drink in the evening?	Lucy drank a gallon of water. Mike drank a liter of water. Who drank more?
Mike drank 2 quarts of water during the day. What are the different amounts that he could have drank throughout the day?	Carla drank some water in the morning and then 2 more cups in the afternoon. She drank a total of 2 quarts of water. How much did she drink in the morning?
Ricky drank 2 quarts of water in the morning, and a pint of water in the afternoon. He drank some more in the evening. He drank a total of 3 quarts. How much did he drink in the evening?	Lucy drank 3 cups of water. Mike drank 1 pint of water. Who drank more and how much more?

Figure 6.8 Visual Introduction

Launch	**Teacher:** Today we are going to work on solving pictorial measurement activities.
	Vocabulary: cup, ounces, quart, gallon
	Math talk: I converted . . .
Model	**Teacher:** We are going to model some problems.
	Carol drank a cup of water in the morning. She drank a pint in the afternoon. She drank a cup in the evening. How much water did she drink altogether? Did she drink more than a quart?
	Kayla: Hmmm . . . I'm going to make everything ounces . . . So a quart is 32 ounces . . . Cup = 8 ounces Pint = 16 ounces Cup = 8 ounces 32 ounces ? ounces <table><tr><td>8</td><td>16</td><td>8</td></tr></table> Cup Pint Cup
Checking for Understanding	**Teacher:** Next Problem
	Jane bought 3 liters of juice. She was going to pour glasses that were 355 ml each. How many glasses can she pour? Estimate first.
	Kayla: I did a bar model. I know a liter is 1000 ml. So she got about 3 cups per liter, which is 9, but she got less, so probably 7 or 8. It's 8 because she doesn't have enough for 9.
	2840 ml
	<table><tr><td>355</td><td>355</td><td>355</td><td>355</td><td>355</td><td>355</td><td>355</td><td>355</td></tr></table>
	8 × 355 *8 × 300 = 2400* *8 × 50 = 400* *8 × 5 = 40* *2400 + 400 + 40 = 2840*

Figure 6.9 Visual Student Activity

	Visual Student Activity
Guided Practice/ Checking for Understanding	**Teacher:** Okay, let's get tricky. I'm going to give you the units and you give me the problem: inches to feet. **Trina:** I bought 30 inches of rope to make bracelets. How many feet of rope did I buy? **Sharon:** That would be 30 divided by 12 . . . which would be 2 feet and 6 inches. 30 inches | 12 inches/1 foot	12 inches/1 foot	6 inches/½ foot	
Set Up for Independent Practice	After everyone has shared, the lesson ends. We are going to be talking more about this in the upcoming days. Are there any questions? What was interesting today? What was tricky?

Figure 6.10 Make Your Own Problem

Make your own conversion problem.
Model it!

Figure 6.11 Lesson Close

Close
♦ What did we do today?   ♦ What was the math we were practicing?   ♦ What concept were we working with?   ♦ Was this easy or tricky?   ♦ Are there any questions?

Figure 6.12 Abstract Introduction

Introduction to Abstract Explorations	
Launch	**Teacher:** Today we are going to continue work on solving measurement word problems **Vocabulary: add to, subtract from, count up, number sentence (equation), liters (l), milliliters (ml), pints (p), cups (c), gram (g), kilogram (kg)** **Math Talk:** ♦ **My strategy _____.** ♦ **I modeled my thinking by _____.** ♦ **I know my answer is correct because _____.**
Model	**Teacher:** I am going to give you some word problems and we will reason them out with different models and tools. Here is one. *Mike made 2.5 liters punch. He put in some more liters. Now he has 4.4 liters. How much did he put in?* **Ted:** Well, if he put in a half liter more, that would make 3 liters and then add 1.4 more liters would be a total of 4.4 liters. So he put in 1.9 liters. <table><tr><td colspan="2" align="center">4.4</td></tr><tr><td>2.5</td><td>?</td></tr></table>
Checking for Understanding	**Teacher: Any other thoughts?** **Connie:** We could subtract 2.5 from 4.4 too. **Teacher:** Yes, we could do that. I am going to read the problem and then you will model it in a part–part–whole diagram and show it to the group. We will take turns explaining our thinking. Here we go.

Figure 6.13 Abstract Student Activity

Abstract Student Activity	
Guided Practice/ Checking for Understanding	The teacher reads different problems. The children solve the problems however they want. They can solve them using different tools and models and show them and explain their thinking to the group. Each time, a different student explains how they solved the problem. _(table: top cell "4"; bottom cells "1.5 liters" and "?")_ **Josephine explains:** I used a part–part–whole mat. The problem said Grandma Mary made 1.5 liters of punch. Then she made some more. Now she has 4.0 liters of punch. How much more did she make? So, I can count up. She put in half a liter more to get to 2 liters and then 2 more liters would be 4 liters. So, she put in 2.5 liters. **Teacher:** Yes. _Everybody models the problems and show it on their part–part–whole mat. Some students have the numbers in the wrong place, and they erase and fix it. The teacher reminds everybody that it is okay to make mistakes because that means you are trying and when you keep trying you will get it._ **Teacher:** We are going to be talking more about this in the upcoming days. Are there any questions? What was interesting today? What was tricky? **Kelly:** I think it is tricky to know where the numbers go. **Teacher:** Yes, it can be tricky. Who can give us some ideas on how to work with the numbers? **Jamal:** You have to look at the total and that goes at the top. The other number is how many there were so that goes in this box. The missing number always goes wherever the part is that you are looking for.
Set Up for Independent Practice	**Jamal:** It depends on what is happening in the problem. **Teacher:** Okay then. Turn and talk with your neighbor about what we did today. You all can go to your next station as soon as I ring the rotation bell.

Figure 6.14 Lesson Close

Close
♦ What did we do today?
♦ What was the math we were practicing?
♦ What were we working on today?
♦ Was this easy or tricky?
♦ Are there any questions?

Figure 6.15 Problem-Solving Cards

500 ml + ? = 4000 ml	Luke made 500 ml of punch. He then put in some cranberry juice. Now he as 4 liters of punch. How much did he put in?
1.7 +? = 3.5	Luke made 1.7 liters of punch. He then added some cranberry juice. Now he as 3 1/2 liters of punch. How much cranberry juice did he put in?
? + 1.6 = 3.20	Luke made punch. First, he put in some orange juice. He then added 1.6 liters of cranberry juice. Now he as 3.20 liters of punch. How much orange juice did he add?
750 ml + ? = 2500 ml	Luke made 750 ml of punch. He then put some cranberry juice. Now he as 2 1/2 liters of punch. How much cranberry juice did he add?
? + 1.8 = 3.5	Jamal made some punch. First, he added some mango juice. Then he added 1.8 liters of orange juice. Now he has 3.5 liters of punch. How much mango juice did he put in?

Section Summary

Measurement problems can be very tricky. Students have to not only work on what is happening in the situation of the problem, but they also are working with understanding metric units of measure and customary units of measure. Start-unknown problems can be very tricky. Many measurement problems should be scaffolded with number lines, part–part–whole models and sketches. The part–part–whole mat is a great abstract visual because students can see the numbers. Number lines and number grids are also great abstract visual scaffolds because students can see the numbers.

Figure 6.16 Overview

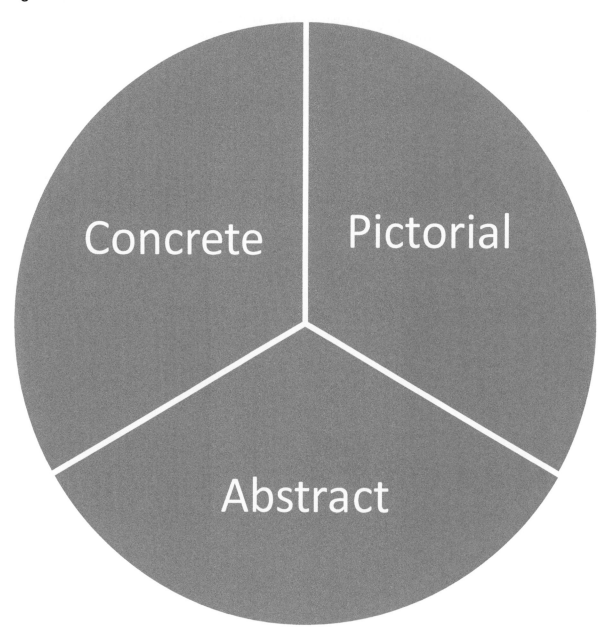

Figure 6.17 Planning Template

Big Idea: Numbers; Operation Meanings & Relationships **Enduring Understanding:** We can model problems in many ways. **Essential Question:** What are the ways to model problems? **I can statement:** I can model problems with different models.	**Materials** ♦ Tools: 1-inch tiles, 1-inch grid paper ♦ Cards ♦ Crayons
Cycle of Engagement **Concrete:** 0.1 0.01 **Pictorial/Drawing:** 0.1 0.01 **Abstract:** 	**Vocabulary & Language Frames** Decimal tile Decimal place-value disk Sketch **My model is . . .** **My strategy is . . .**

Figure 6.18 Differentiation

3 Differentiated Lessons

In this series of lessons, students are working on the concept of decimals. They are developing this concept through concrete activities, pictorial activities and abstract activities. Everybody should do the cycle. Some students progress through it more quickly than others. Here are some things to think about as you do these lessons.

Emergent	On Grade Level	Above Grade Level
Students need to understand one step problems. Make sure that students understand the idea of problem solving, solving one way and checking another. Make sure that you as the teacher have scaffolded the problems.	Students should be comfortable using different models. So do lots of this work where students are modeling it and explaining their work.	Extend the number range.

 Looking for Misunderstandings and Common Errors

They need to take their time and use various models to act out and model the problems. Use hundredths grids, place-value disks, decimal tiles and decimal number charts.

Figure 6.19 Anchor Chart

Solving Multiplication Word Problems With Tape Diagrams

The candy store sold chocolate bars for $1.25. How much did 3 candy bars cost?

Concrete

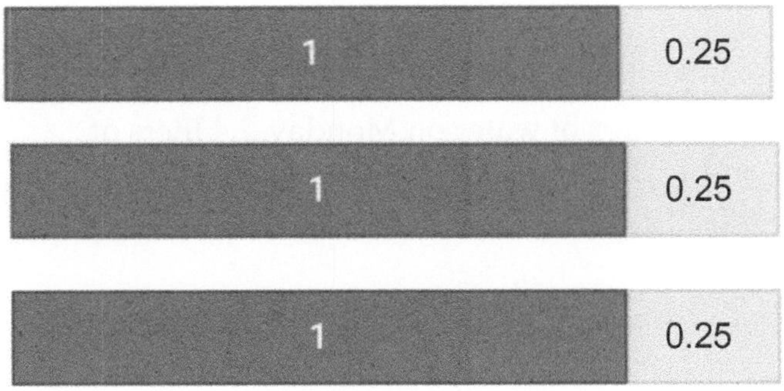
1
0.25
1
0.25
1
0.25

Sketch

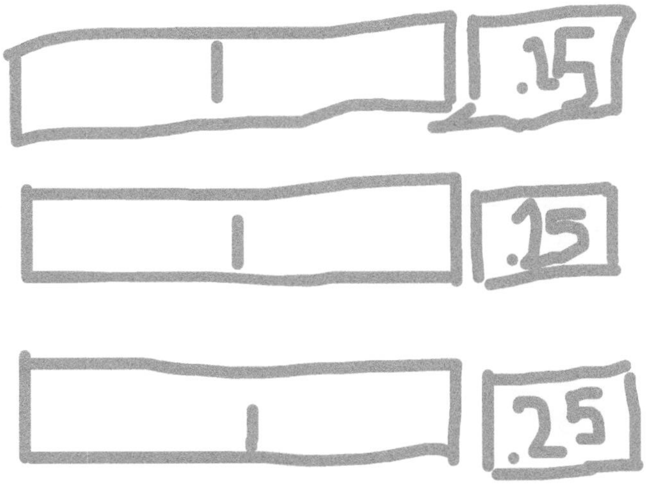
1
.15
1
.25
1
.25

Abstract
$1.25
$1.25
<u>$1.25</u>
$3.75

Figure 6.20 Concrete Introduction

Introduction to Concrete Explorations

Launch	**Teacher:** Today we are going to work on word problems with decimals.
	
	Vocabulary: product, factor, multiply, divisor, dividend, quotient, compare, as many as
	
	Math Talk:
	    The answer is . . .
	    My model is . . .

Model	**Teacher:** Luke drank 1.5 liters of water on Monday, 2.4 liters of water on Tuesday and 1.7 liters of water on Wednesday. How much did he drink in 3 days? **Claire:** 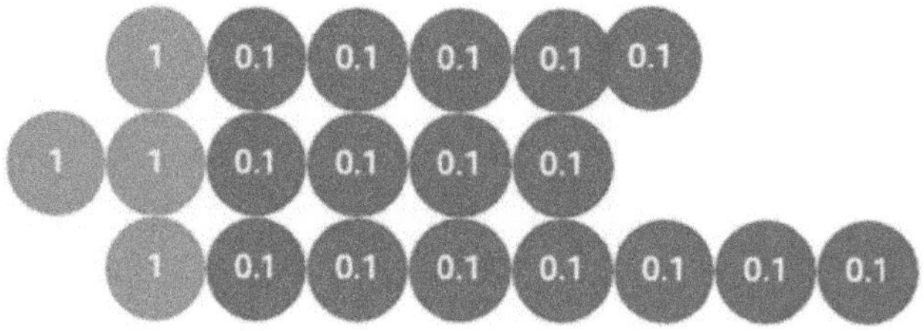 He drank 4 liters plus 1.6 more liters. The total was 5.6 liters,
Checking for Understanding	**Teacher:** Who modeled it another way? **Ted:** I used decimal tiles. I also got 5.6 liters. 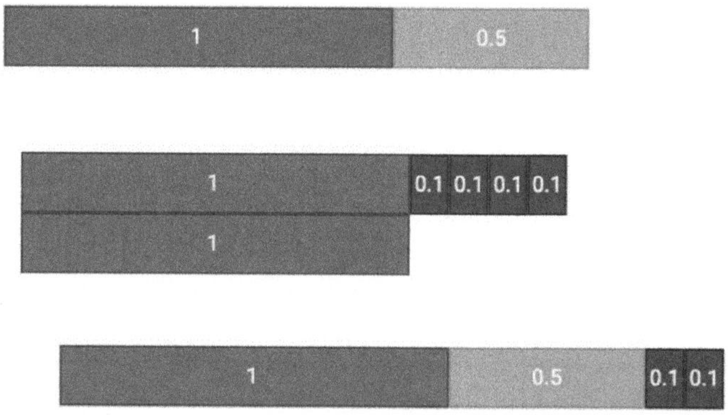

Figure 6.21 Concrete Student Activity

	Concrete Student Activity
Guided Practice/ Checking for Understanding	The teacher passes out the problems. Students pull a card and act out their problems. The students each get a chance to share their problem and explain how they solved it. **Tami:** My problem is this: The toy store sold marbles for $.25 each. Kay bought 5. How much did she spend? She spent $1.25. | 0.25	0.25	0.25	0.25	0.25	
Set Up for Independent Practice	Every child shares their problem and how they solved it. **Teacher:** We are going to be talking more about this in the upcoming days. Turn and talk to your neighbor about the math we did today. What was interesting today? What was tricky?

Figure 6.22 Lesson Close

Close
◆ What did we do today? ◆ What was the math we were practicing? ◆ What was the math we were focusing on today? ◆ Was this easy or tricky? ◆ Are there any questions?

Figure 6.23 Multiplication Comparison Cards

The bakery had 8 lemon cookies. They sold them for $0.55 each. How much did 8 cost?	The bakery had 12 vanilla cookies. They sold them for $0.59 each. How much did they cost?
The bakery had 9 apple pies. They sold them for $5.35 each. How much did they cost?	The bakery had 3 chocolate cakes. They sold them for $7.85 each. How much did they cost?
The bakery had 2 mini cherry pies. They sold them for $2.35 each. How much did they cost?	The bakery had 10 chocolate cupcakes. They sold them for $0.85 each. How much did they cost?

Figure 6.24 Visual Introduction

	Introduction to Visual Explorations
Launch	**Teacher:** Today we are going to continue to work on solving word problems and modeling them. **Vocabulary:** multiplication, word problem, product, factor, dividend, quotient, divisor **Math Talk:** My strategy was . . . My model was . . .
Model	Teacher: Here is the problem. **The bakery sold 3 mini cookies for $.50 each. How much did they cost altogether?** **Penelope:** I used my coins. It's $1.50. 
Checking for Understanding	This conversation continues with the students using models to solve the problems.

Figure 6.25 Visual Student Activity

Visual Student Activity

Guided Practice/ Checking for Understanding	The teacher passes out word problem cards. Students pull a card and model their problems. The students each get a chance to share their problem and explain how they solved it. **Maria: My problem is this:** | The toy store sold marbles for \$0.25 each. Maria bought 10. How much did she pay? | **Maria:** Here is my model. I used coins grouped them in dollar amounts.  **Teacher:** Does everybody see that? Who can explain what Maria just did? **Clyde:** She used money. It's easy to think about quarters in this problem.
Set Up for Independent Practice	Teacher gives everybody a chance to do and discuss a problem. After everyone has shared the lesson ends. "We are going to be talking more about this in the upcoming days. Are there any questions? What was interesting today? What was tricky?"

Figure 6.26 Lesson Close

Close
◆ What did we do today?
◆ What was the math we were practicing?
◆ What were we working on today?
◆ Was this easy or tricky?
◆ Are there any questions?

Figure 6.27 Tape Diagram Cards

The toy store sold marbles for 20 cents each. How much did 10 cost?	The toy store sold marbles for 35 cents each. How much did 5 cost?
The toy store sold marbles for 25 cents each. How much did 8 cost?	The toy store sold marbles for 40 cents each. How much did 7 cost?
The toy store sold marbles for 50 cents each. How much did 10 cost?	The toy store sold marbles for 50 cents each. How much did 12 cost?
The toy store sold marbles for 10 cents each. How much did 10 cost?	The toy store sold marbles for 75 cents each. How much did 4 cost?

Figure 6.28 Abstract Introduction

Introduction to Abstract Explorations	
Launch	**Teacher:** Today we are going to work on making up word problems. **Vocabulary:** decimals, tenths, hundredths, thousandths **Math Talk:** The whole is _____. One part is ____. The other part is _____.
Model	**Teacher:** The answer was $1.25. What was the question? **Yesenia:** I bought 5 marbles. They were 25 cents each. How much did they cost? I could model it with quarters. **Gary:** Joe had $2.00. He bought some gum for 75 cents. How much did he have left? Here's my model.
Checking for Understanding	**Teacher:** Okay, great start. Who else wants to give us an answer and we will think of the question? **Mike:** The answer is $0.75. What is the question? **Maria:** I had 1 dollar. I bought a marble for 25 cents. How much do I have left?

Figure 6.29 Abstract Student Activity

	Abstract Student Activity
Guided Practice/ Checking for Understanding	**Teacher:** Let's continue. Who has other questions for 75 cents? **Leah:** I had $2.00. I bought a soda for $1.25. How much did I get back? **Trina:** I had $3.00. I bought a sandwich for $2.25. How much did I get back?
Set Up for Independent Practice	After the discussion, the teacher asks the students what was easy and what was tricky.

Figure 6.30 Lesson Close

Close
◆ What did we do today? ◆ What was the math we were practicing? ◆ What were we studying today? ◆ Was this easy or tricky? ◆ Are there any questions?

Figure 6.31 Word problem cards

The answer is 75 cents. What is the question?	The answer is 85 cents. What is the question?	The answer is 70 cents. What is the question?	The answer is 25 cents. What is the question?
The answer is 55 cents. What is the question?	The answer is 45 cents. What is the question?	The answer is 15 cents. What is the question?	The answer is 5 cents. What is the question?

Section Summary

In this section, we discussed modeling decimal problems. Students should work with a variety of models, including fraction tiles, decimal tiles, decimal wheels, decimal grids, decimal number lines and decimal grids. Students should have to solve problems and make them up. Students must explain their thinking. They should solve the problem one way and check it another.

Figure 6.32 Overview

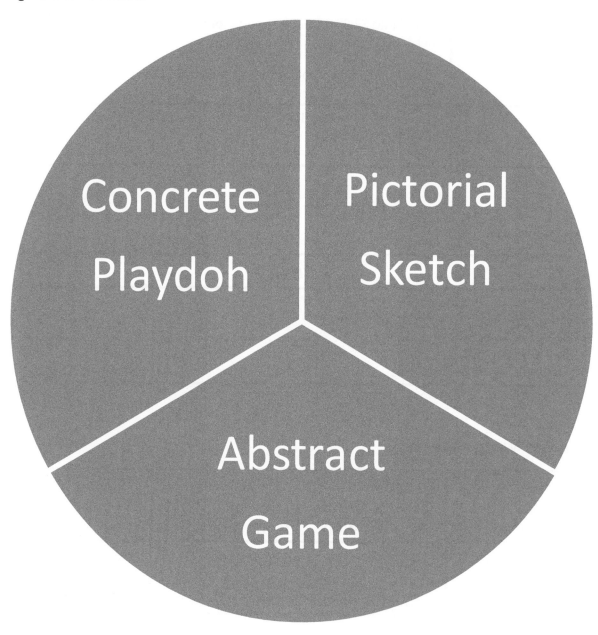

Figure 6.33 Planning Template

Dividing a Fraction by a Whole Number

Big Idea: Operation Meanings & Relationships

Enduring Understanding: We can model problems in many ways.

Essential Question: What are the ways to model fraction division problems?

I can statement: I can model and solve fraction division problems.

Materials
- Tools: playdough
- Paper
- Pencils/Crayons

Cycle of Engagement
Concrete:

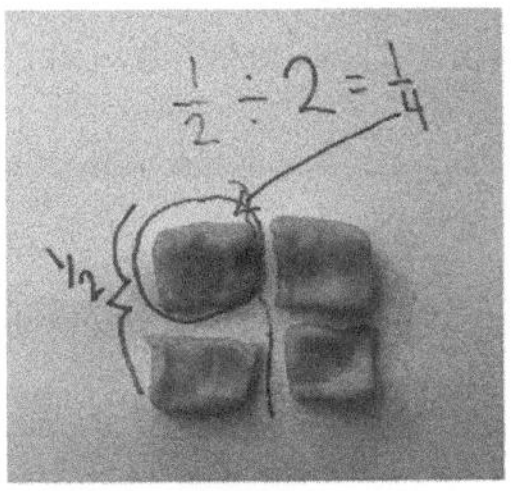

Pictorial:

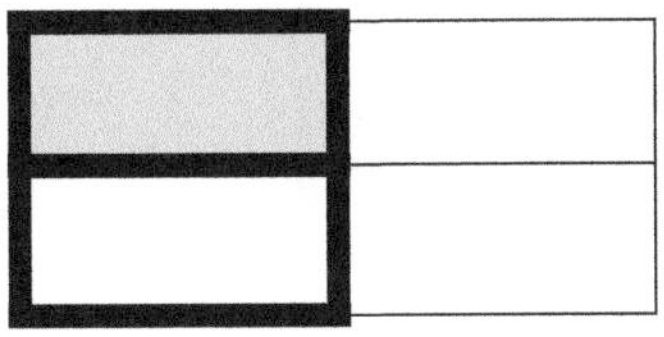

Abstract
$1/2 \div 2 = 1/4$

Vocabulary & Language Frames

Fraction	Dividend
Whole Number	Divisor
Numerator	Quotient
Denominator	Model

Math Talk:
- My strategy was _____.
- My model was _____.

Figure 6.34 Differentiation

3 Differentiated Lessons
In this series of lessons, students are working on fraction division problems. They are developing this concept through concrete activities, pictorial activities and abstract activities. Everybody should do the cycle. Some students progress through it more quickly than others. Here are some things to think about as you do these lessons.

Emerging	On Grade Level	Above Grade Level
Review division. As you introduce this to students, do a lot of work by modeling it in different ways.	The standard in many states is that students can divide a unit fraction by a whole number and a whole number by a unit fraction.	Extend the number range.

 Looking for Misunderstandings and Common Errors

Students often find dividing a fraction by a whole number a bit tricky. Spend a great deal of time on developing the concept. Use playdough so that students have to cut, model and explain their thinking. Use fraction tiles and circles.

Figure 6.35 Anchor Chart

Solving Fraction Division Problems

Concrete

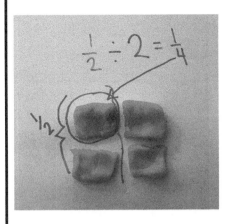

Pictorial $\frac{1}{2} \div 2 = \frac{1}{4}$

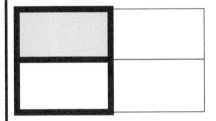

Abstract

$\frac{1}{2} \div 2 = \frac{1}{4}$

Figure 6.36 Concrete Introduction

\multicolumn{2}{c|}{**Introduction to Concrete Explorations**}	
Launch	**Teacher:** Today we are going to work on dividing fractions. **Vocabulary:** fraction, whole number, numerator, denominator, divisor, dividend, quotient, model **Math Talk:** My model is _____.
Model	**Teacher:** Listen to this problem. Clark had 1/2 of a pizza left. He split it with his 2 friends. What fraction of the pizza did each person get? **Tami:** I built a model. I cut it in half. Then I divided it into 3 pieces. I got that each person got 1/6 of the pizza. (Tami's half) **(The other part of the pizza)**
Checking for Understanding	**Teacher:** Listen to this problem. Clark had ½ of a pizza left. He split it equally between his 3 friends and himself What fraction of the pizza did each person get? **Tami:** I built a model. I cut it in half. Then I divided it into 4 pieces. I got that each person got 1/8 of the pizza. One half of the pizza The other half of the pizza

Figure 6.37 Concrete Student Activity

	Concrete Student Activity
Guided Practice/ Checking for Understanding	**Teacher:** Listen to this problem. Clark had 1/2 of a pizza left. He split it with his sister. What fraction of the pizza did each person get? **Tami:** I built a model. I cut it in half. Then I divided it by 2 people. I got that each person got 1/4 of the pizza. **(Half the pizza)** 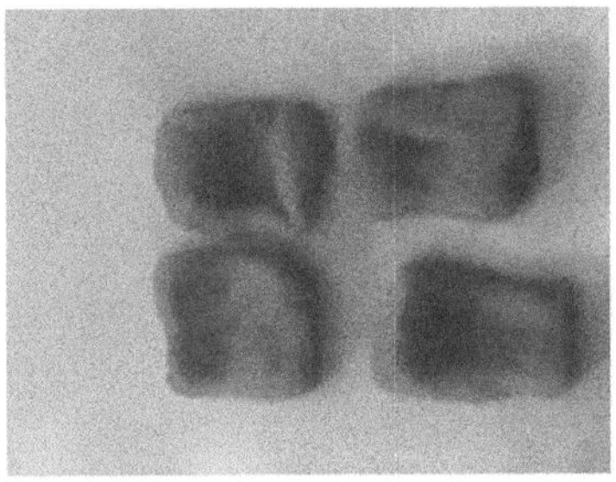 **(Other half of the pizza)**
Set Up for Independent Practice	Every child shares out their problem and how they solved it. We are going to be talking more about that in the upcoming days. Turn and tell your neighbor what it means to divide a fraction by a whole number. What was interesting today? What was tricky?

Figure 6.38 Lesson Close

Close
◆ What did we do today? ◆ What was the math we were practicing? ◆ What were we doing today? ◆ Was this easy or tricky? ◆ Are there any questions?

Figure 6.39 Visual Introduction

Introduction to Visual Explorations

Launch	**Teacher:** Today we are going to work on dividing fractions. **Vocabulary:** fraction, whole number, numerator, denominator, divisor, dividend, quotient, model **Math Talk:** My model is _____.
Model	**Teacher:** Listen to this problem. Clark had 1/2 of a pizza left. He split it with his sister. What fraction of the pizza did each person get? **Tami:** I drew a model. I cut it in half. Then I divided it by 2 people. I got that each person got 1/4 of the whole pizza. 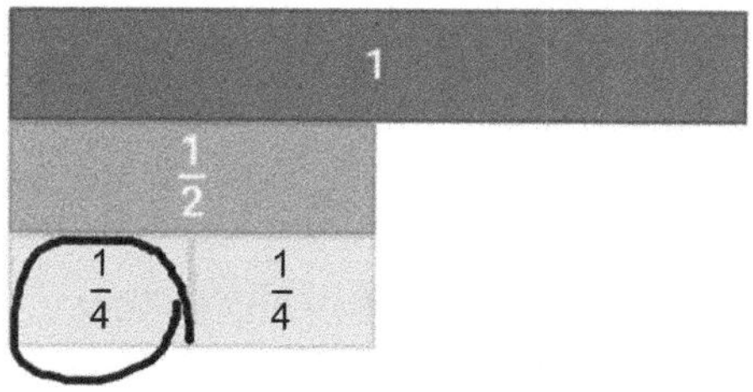
Checking for Understanding	**Teacher:** Listen to this problem. Clark had 1/2 of a pizza left. He split it with 2 cousins. What fraction of the pizza did each person get? **Tony:** Each person got 1/6 of the pizza. I drew a pizza. Cut it in half. Divided the half between 3 people. 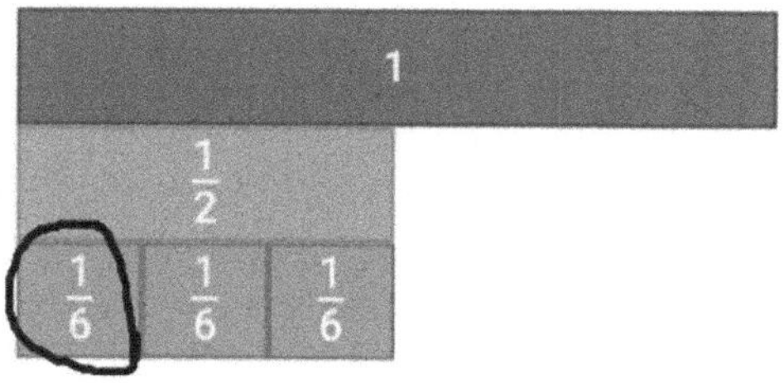

Figure 6.40 Visual Student Activity

	Visual Student Activity
Guided Practice/ Checking for Understanding	**Teacher:** Listen to this problem. Clark had 1/2 of a pizza left. He split it with 3 of his friends. What fraction of the pizza did each person get?
	Tami: I drew a model. I cut it in half. Then I divided it by 4 people. I got that each person got 1/8 of the pizza. 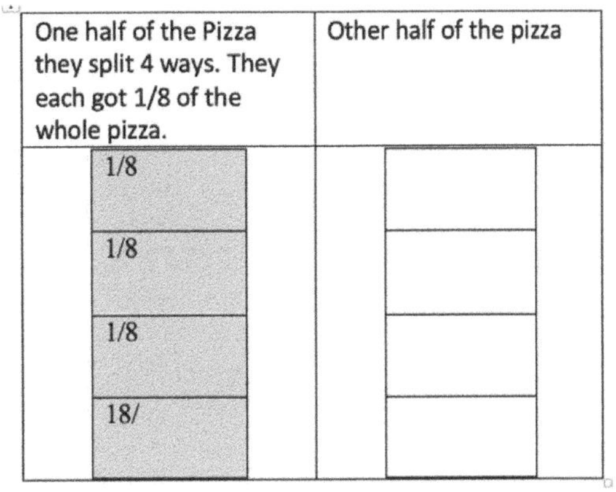
	<table><tr><td>One half of the Pizza they split 4 ways. They each got 1/8 of the whole pizza.</td><td>Other half of the pizza</td></tr><tr><td>1/8 1/8 1/8 18/</td><td></td></tr></table>
Set Up for Independent Practice	Every child shares out their problem and how they solved it on the part–part–whole mat. We are going to be talking more about that in the upcoming days. Are there any questions? What was interesting today? What was tricky?

Figure 6.41 Lesson Close

Close
◆ What did we do today?   ◆ What was the math we were practicing?   ◆ What were we doing today?   ◆ Was this easy or tricky?   ◆ Are there any questions?

Figure 6.42 Abstract Introduction

	Introduction to Abstract Activities
Launch	**Teacher:** Today we are going to work on dividing fractions. **Vocabulary:** fraction, whole number, numerator, denominator, divisor, dividend, quotient, model **Math Talk:** My model is _____.
Model	**Teacher:** Today we are going to play a board game where you have to solve a division problem. You can use your paper and pencil to calculate. **Division** Instructions: Spin the spinner. Whoever has the lowest number goes first. Move that many spaces and pick a card and solve the problem.. The first person to land on finish wins. FINISH START
Checking for Understanding	**Teacher:** Who wants to read one of the cards? Carol: 4 kids split 1/2 of a pizza. What fraction of the pizza did each kid get? I got a card that said 4 kids split half a pizza. Each kid would get 1/8 of the pizza. **Teacher:** How do you know? **Carol:** I drew the model.

Figure 6.43 Abstract Student Activity

	Abstract Student Activity
Guided Practice/ Checking for Understanding	**Teacher:** Who wants to do another one. Carl: [5 kids split 1/2 of a pizza. What fraction of the pizza did each kid get?] I got a card that 5 kids split half a pizza. Each kid got 1/10 of the pizza. **Teacher:** How do you know? **Catherine:** I did an equation.
Set Up for Independent Practice	The teacher continues to watch the groups as they work on solving their problems. When everyone has finished the teacher asks the students to explain their thinking. The teacher also asks them what was easy and what was tricky.

Figure 6.44 Lesson Close

Close
♦ What did we do today? ♦ What was the math we were practicing? ♦ What were we doing today? ♦ Was this easy or tricky? ♦ Are there any questions?

Figure 6.45 Word Problem Cards

4 kids split 1/2 of a pizza. What fraction of the pizza did each kid get?	5 kids split 1/2 of a pizza. What fraction of the pizza did each kid get?
2 kids split 1/2 of a pizza. What fraction of the pizza did each kid get?	3 kids split 1/2 of a pizza. What fraction of the pizza did each kid get?
4 kids split 1/3 of a pizza. What fraction of the pizza did each kid get?	5 kids split 1/2 of a pizza. What fraction of the pizza did each kid get?
3 kids split 1/3 of a pizza. What fraction of the pizza did each kid get?	4 kids split 3/4 of a pizza. What fraction of the pizza did each kid get?
2 kids split 1/3 of a pizza. What fraction of the pizza did each kid get?	2 kids split 3/6 of a pizza. What fraction of the pizza did each kid get?

Figure 6.46 Division Game

Division

Instructions: Spin the spinner. Whoever has the lowest number goes first. Move that many spaces and pick a card and solve the problem.. The first person to land on finish wins.

Section Summary

Dividing a fraction by a whole number is a tricky concept for many students. It is important that students understand conceptually what they are doing. Tell stories with small numbers so that students can imagine the story. They need to be able to wrap their minds around the number so in the beginning the numbers should be something that they can envision like halves, thirds or fourths. Acting it out with playdough gives a kinesthetic aspect to the concept. Students get to own the knowledge because they have acted it out with the playdough. They should then go on to draw it and then to learn how to solve it algorithmically.

Figure 6.47 3-Read Problems Planning Template

3-Read Problems	
Big Idea: We can use different strategies and models to solve word problems. **Enduring Understanding:** Students will understand how to model problems in many ways. **Essential Question:** What are the ways to model this type of problem? **I can statement:** I can use tools to model my thinking.	**Materials** ♦ Problem-Solving Mats ♦ Cards ♦ Crayons

Cycle of Engagement
 	
Concrete-Pictorial-Abstract
 	
In this type of problem, the class chorally reads the problem 3 times. The first time the class reads the problem, they focus on what is happening in the problem. The second time, they focus on what the numbers mean. The third time, they focus on asking questions about the problems.
	Vocabulary & Language Frames
	♦ Strategies
	♦ Models
	♦ Tools
	
	Math Talk
	    My strategy was . . .
	    My model was . . .
	
	Mathematical Processes/Practices
	♦ Problem-Solving
	♦ Reasoning
	♦ Modeling
	♦ Tools

Figure 6.48 3-Read Word Problems Anchor Chart

3-Read Word Problem

We can read a problem 3 times.

The first time we read it and think about the situation.
What is the story about? Who is in it? What is happening?

The second time we read it and think about the numbers.
What are the numbers? What do they mean? What might we do with those numbers in this situation?

The third time we read it and think about what questions we could ask.
What do we notice in this story? What do we wonder? What do we want to ask about this story?

The Jones family went on vacation. They drove 167 miles on both Monday and Tuesday. They drove 99 miles each of the next 3 days in a row.

First Read: What is this story about? It is about a family who went on vacation.

Second Read: What do the numbers mean? They tell us how far they drove.

Third Read: What could we ask about this story?

How far did they drive altogether?
How far did they drive round trip?
Did they drive farther the first 2 days or the last 3 days?

Figure 6.49 3-Read Word Problems Lesson

Launch	**Teacher:** Today we are going to work on word problems. We are going to do a 3-read, like the ones we do in whole group. **Vocabulary:** model, strategy **Math Talk:** ♦ My strategy was . . . ♦ My model was . . .
Model	*Story: Mike had a candy bar. He ate 1/3 of it. His brother ate ¼ of it. His friend Tom ate the rest.* *First Read: What is this story about?* It is about Mike sharing his candy bar. *Second Read: What do the numbers mean?* Mike ate 1/3 of it. His brother ate 1/4. His friend ate the rest. *Third Read: What could we ask about this story?* ♦ Who ate the most? ♦ Who ate the least? ♦ How much did his friend eat?
Checking for Understanding	*Teacher: Okay, pick 2 questions and answer them. We will come back in a few minutes to discuss them. . . . Who answered question 1? Tell us your strategy and show us a model of your thinking.*
Guided Practice/ Checking for Understanding	*Tina: Well we have to find a common denominator to add 1/3 and ¼ and that is 12. So Mike ate the most.* *Teacher: Okay, who did question 2?* *Erica: His brother ate the least.*
Set Up for Independent Practice	Students continue to share their thinking with the group. When they are done the teacher facilitates a conversation about what the math was for the day and then what students thought was easy and what they thought was tricky.

Figure 6.50 Lesson Close

Close
♦ What did we do today? ♦ What was the math we were practicing? ♦ Was this easy or tricky? ♦ Are there any questions?

Figure 6.51 3-Read Cards

Mike had a candy bar. He ate 1/3 of it. His brother ate 1/4 of it. His friend Tom ate the rest.	*Marta had a candy bar. She ate 1/2 of it. Her brother ate 1/3 of it. Her friend Tori ate the rest.*
Jamal had a candy bar. He ate 1/3 of it. His brother ate 1/3 of it. His friend Tom ate 1/6 of it. His other friend Kelli ate the rest.	*Mabel had a candy bar. She ate 2/4 of it. Her brother ate 3/8 of it. Her friend Tami ate the rest.*
Hong had a candy bar. He ate 2/4 of it. His brother ate 2/8 of it. His friend Tom ate the rest.	*Kelli had a candy bar. She ate 5/10 of it. Her sister ate 2/5 of it. Her friend Tomasina ate the rest.*
Mike had a candy bar. He ate 1/4 of it. His brother ate 2/8 of it. His friend Tom ate the rest.	*Sharon had a candy bar. She ate 3/6 of it. Her sister ate 1/3 of it. Her friend Tori ate the rest.*

Figure 6.52 Picture Prompt Planning Template

Picture Prompt Word Problems

Big Idea: Word problems are a part of our everyday lives.

Enduring Understanding: Students will understand that they can model problems in many ways. There are also many different strategies to solve them.

Essential Question: Where do we see word problems in real life?

I can statement: I can model problems.

Materials
♦ Tools: Manipulatives
♦ Templates
♦ Cards
♦ Crayons

Questions
♦ What is your strategy?
♦ What is your model?
♦ Why does that work?
♦ How can you show that?

Cycle of Engagement

Picture

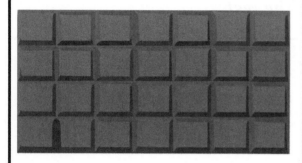

Equation:

$4 \times 7 = 28$

Vocabulary & Language Frames

Add, subtract, take away, sum, difference

My strategy was . . .

My model was . . .

Math Processes/Practices
♦ Problem-Solving
♦ Reasoning
♦ Models
♦ Tools

Figure 6.53 Picture Prompt Word Problem Lesson

Picture Prompt Word Problems	
Launch	Teacher: Today we are going to work on word problems. We are going to do a picture prompt word problem today. Vocabulary: model, strategy Math Talk: ♦ My strategy was . . . ♦ My model was . . .
Model	Teacher: Today we are going to look at pictures and tell word problems. Let's think about some word problems for this picture. Luke: Sue gave her brother 1/2 of her candy bar? How many pieces did he get? Marta: I know the answer . . . 14 pieces. Because there are 28 pieces total.
Checking for Understanding	Ted: I have another one. Mike gave his brother 1/7 of his candy bar. How many pieces did he give his brother? Kelly: I know . . . 4 because if you break this up into 7 parts . . . each of those parts has 4 pieces.
Guided Practice/ Checking for Understanding	Teacher: Who has another question? Jamal: Chloe gave 1/4 of the candy bar to her cousin. How many pieces did her cousin get? Tami: Her brother got 7 pieces.
Set Up for Independent Practice	Teacher: Okay. Who's next? The teacher goes around the circle, and everyone gets a chance to share their stories. They then wrap up and go to workstations.

Figure 6.54 Open Word Problems Lesson

Open Word Problems Lesson	
Launch	**Teacher:** Today we are going to work on word problems. **Vocabulary:** model, strategy, tool, sum, difference, addend **Math Talk:** ♦ My strategy was . . . ♦ My model was . . .
Model	**Teacher:** The answer is 1/4 of a pound of strawberries. What is the question? **Terry:** I know. Mom bought a pound of strawberries. The kids ate 3/4 of it. How much is left? **Kayla:** I could say Grandma made a cake. She used 1/8 of a pound of strawberries in the mix and 1/8 of a pound of strawberries for the frosting. What fraction of a pound did she use altogether? **Teacher:** Absolutely. All of these work. Can you both draw a model of what you said?
Checking for Understanding	**Teacher:** Do other people have some ideas? **Jamal:** Auntie June had a half a pan of brownies. The kids ate 1/2 of the 1/2. How much is left?
Guided Practice/ Checking for Understanding	**Teacher:** Okay, let's say the answer was 3.5 liters of lemonade. What is the question? **Hong:** Grandpa had 5 liters of lemonade. He drank 1.5 liters. How much does he have left? **Tami:** Sue had 7 liters of lemonade. The kids drank 3.5 liters. How much is left?
Set Up for Independent Practice	**Teacher:** Okay. Who's next? The teacher goes around the circle, and everyone gets a chance to share their stories. They then wrap up and go to workstations.

Section Summary

It is important to do open questions with students where they have to contextualize numbers. This is part of the mathematical practices and processes (NGA Center & CCSSO, 2010). We want students to be able to reason about numbers. We want students to be able to tell stories not only solve them. Giving them rich structures to do that is vital.

Depth of Knowledge

Depth of Knowledge (DoK) is a framework that encourages us to ask questions that require that students think, reason, explain, defend and justify their thinking (Webb, 2002). Here is snapshot of what that can look like in terms of word problem work.

Figure 6.55 DoK Activities

	What are different strategies and models that we can use to solve measurement problems?	What are different strategies and models to model multidigit multiplication problems ?	What are different strategies and models that we can use to solve fraction division problems?
DoK Level 1 (These are questions for which students are required to simply recall/reproduce an answer/do a procedure.)	Solve. Write a setup equation (with a symbol for the unknown) and a solution equation. Grandma used 740 ml of apple juice, 568 ml of orange juice and 499 ml of pineapple juice, in her fruit punch. How much fruit punch did she make altogether in liters?	Solve: The farm stand sold 12 baskets with 60 apples in each one. How many apples did they sell altogether?	Solve: Grandma had 1/2 of pan of brownies left. She split it between her 3 grandchildren. How much did each child get?

Figure 6.55 (Continued)

DoK Level 2 (These are questions for which students have to use information, think about concepts and reason.) This is considered a more challenging problem than a level 1 problem.	Solve and model in two different ways. Explain your thinking. Grandma made 2 liters of fruit punch. She used 340 ml of apple juice, 267 ml of orange juice and the rest was pineapple juice. How much orange juice did she use?	Write a word problem where you multiply using two 2-digit numbers, and the answer is in between 400 and 450.	Solve: Mike had a candy bar. He ate 1/2 of it. He gave his cousin 1/4 of it and his friend the rest of it. What are some questions you could ask about this problem? Solve them.
DoK Level 3 (These are questions for which students have to reason, plan, explain, justify and defend their thinking.)	Solve. Grandma made some fruit punch. She used apple, orange and pineapple juice. She made 1 liter of punch altogether. What are some possible combinations of the juice that she could have made. Defend your answer. Prove that it is correct by solving one way and checking another.	Solve. The answer is 452 marbles. What is the question?.	Write a word problem where you have to divide a fraction by a whole number.

A great resource for asking open questions is Marion Small's Good Questions: Great ways to differentiate mathematics instruction in the standards-based classroom (2017). Also Robert Kaplinsky has done a great job in pushing our thinking forward with the Depth of Knowledge Matrices he created (https://robertkaplinsky.com/depth-knowledge-matrix-elementary-math/). The Kentucky Department of Education also has a great DoK math matrix (2007).

Figure 6.56 Asking Rigorous Questions

DoK 1	DoK 2 At this level, students explain their thinking.	DoK 3 At this level students, have to justify, defend and prove their thinking with objects, drawings and diagrams.
What is the answer to . . . Can you model the problem? Can you identify the answer that matches this equation?	How do you know that the equation is correct? Can you pick the correct answer and explain why it is correct? How can you model that problem in more than one way? What is another way to model that problem? Can you model that on the . . . Give me an example of a . . . type of problem. Which answer is incorrect? Explain your thinking.	Can you prove that your answer is correct? Prove that . . . Explain why that is the answer . . . Show me how to solve that and explain what you are doing.

Key Points

♦ Measurement Problems
♦ Multiplication Tile and Tape Diagram Problems
♦ Picture Prompts
♦ 3-Read Problems
♦ Open Word Problems

Chapter Summary

It is important to work with students in small guided math groups focusing on word problems. Word problems have a learning trajectory (Carpenter, Fennema, Franke, Levi, & Empson, 1999, 2015). Most states have outlined the word problem types that each grade level is responsible for in their standards. In a guided math group, the goal is to work with students around the word problem types that they are learning.

Students are usually at different levels when learning word problems. They are scaffolded into a hierarchy that goes from easy to challenging. By 5th grade, students dive deep into all 9 types of multiplication and division word problems, as well as measurement problems. Measurement is often difficult for students, and that is why it is so important to give students an opportunity to work in small groups to experience the math and actually to do the measurements.

The small-group discussion should reference the whole-group problem-solving work. The focus should be on getting students to think about the context and the numbers, reason about the problem and use visual representations and tools to unpack it. Students should have to write an equation with a symbol for the unknown and solve one way and check another.

Problem-solving should be done throughout the year, in different parts of math workshop, during the introduction, in math workstations, sometimes in guided math groups and sometimes for homework.

Reflection Questions

1. How are you currently teaching word problem lessons?
2. Are you making sure that you do concrete, pictorial and abstract activities?
3. What do your students struggle with the most and what ideas are you taking away from this chapter that might inform your work?

References

Carpenter, T. P., Fennema, E., Franke, M. L., Levi, L., & Empson, S. B. (2015). *Children's Mathematics: Cognitively Guided Instruction*. Portsmouth, NH: Heinemann.

Kentucky Department of Education. (2007). Support Materials for Core Content for Assessment Version 4.1 Mathematics. Retrieved on January 15, 2017, from the internet.

National Governors Association Center for Best Practices & Council of Chief State School Officers. (2010). *Common Core State Standards for Mathematics (CCSSM)*. Washington, DC: Authors.

Schoenfeld, A. H. (1991). On Mathematics as Sense-Making: An Informal Attack on the Unfortunate Divorce of Formal and Informal Mathematics. In J. F. Voss, D. N. Perkins, & J. W. Segal (Eds.), *Informal Reasoning and Education* (pp. 311–343). Hillsdale, NJ: Lawrence Erlbaum Associates.

Smalls, M. (2017). *Good Questions: Great Ways to Differentiate Mathematics Instructions* (3rd edition). New York: TC Press.

Stacey, K., & MacGregor, M. (1999). Learning the algebraic method of solving problems. The Journal of Mathematical Behavior, 18(2), 149–167. https://doi.org/10.1016/S0732-3123(99)00026-7.

Verschaffel, L., Greer, B., & De Corte, E. (2000). *Making Sense of Word Problems*. Lisse, The Netherlands: Swets & Zeitlinger.

7
Fraction Guided Math Lessons

Worldwide, students have trouble with fractions. Yet, fractions are foundational to understanding other aspects of mathematics. Researchers emphasize the key to getting students to understand fractions is to build on conceptual understanding. If students have conceptual understanding, then when they have to learn and use procedural knowledge, it makes it that much easier because they understand what they are doing.

In the primary grades, the conceptual understanding foundation is being laid. In 3rd grade, there must be an emphasis on understanding fractions as equal sized pieces of a whole, plotting a fraction on a number line and beginning concepts of equivalence. In 4th grade, students learn to compose and decompose fractions, add and subtract them with the same denominator, find equivalent fractions, and, in some states, learn to multiply them by whole numbers. When the emphasis is not placed on the teaching and learning of fractions, students walk away with misunderstandings and misconceptions that grow and impede the learning of more difficult fraction concepts in later grades. One of the biggest misconceptions that students carry with them is viewing the numerator and the denominator as separate numbers rather than 1 number.

Research shows that young children can understand basic fraction concepts such as sharing and the size of fractions when they are set in real-life contexts. Given real contexts, students can develop a fundamental understanding of ordering fractions and equivalence in 3rd grade and solidify this understanding of these concepts in By 5th grade they are ready to explore addition and subtraction of fractions with unlike denominators and multiplication and division of fractions. It is very important to contextualize the discussion about fractions so that students have stories to understand the concepts. We must try to connect students' "intuitive knowledge to formal fraction concepts" (Fazio & Seigler, n.d).

It is also important to start introducing formal fraction names and attach them to the models and have students do drawings and sketches of these fractions with labels. Fraction notation is important, and we don't want students to be afraid of it, so we should give them plenty of opportunities to write and name the fractions. We should spend a great deal of time building conceptual understanding by doing measurement activities, number lines and comparing activities based on real-life situations. We can use measuring string for jewelry making, talking about sharing food and using rulers. We can use measuring cups, measuring tapes and rulers to model real-life situations.

DOI: 10.4324/9781003169666-7

Research Note 🔍

Students struggle with fractions. On a national test, only 50% of American 8th graders correctly ordered three fractions from smallest to largest (National Council of Teachers of Mathematics, 2007). Students confuse whole numbers and fractions and often assume what is true for whole numbers is true for fractions even through high school (Vamvakoussi & Vosniadou, 2010). Children should be introduced to fractions at an early age, making connections to their informal intuitive understanding of sharing and proportionality (Fazio & Siegler, n.d.; Empson, 1999).

Adding Fractions with Unlike Denominators

Figure 7.1 Overview

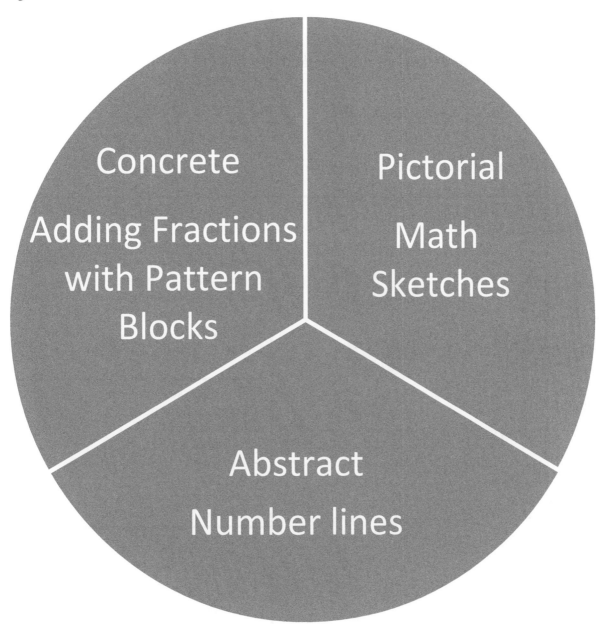

Figure 7.2 Planning Template

Adding Fractions	
Big Idea: Numbers, Equivalence, Operation Meanings and Relationships **Enduring Understanding:** Students will understand that adding fractions can be modeled in many different ways. **Essential Question:** Why are fractions important? How do we use them in real life? **I can statement:** I can add fractions using many different models.	**Materials** ♦ Tools: Fraction Strips, Pattern Blocks ♦ Templates: Fraction Strip Template ♦ Crayons ♦ Paper

Cycle of Engagement
Concrete: 2/5 + 3/10

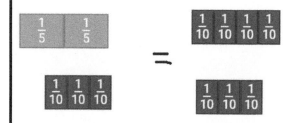

Pictorial: 2/5 + 3/10

1 Whole									
1/2					1/2				
1/3			1/3			1/3			
1/4		1/4		1/4			1/4		
1/5		1/5		1/5		1/5		1/5	
1/10	1/10	1/10	1/10	1/10	1/10	1/10	1/10	1/10	1/10

Vocabulary & Language Frames

Vocabulary: halves, thirds, fourths, fifths, sixths, eighths, tenths, twelfths, denominator, numerator, whole number, sum, addends

Math Talk:
I added ___ and ___. My sum is ___.

Math Processes/Practices
♦ Problem-Solving
♦ Reasoning
♦ Models
♦ Tools
♦ Precision
♦ Structure
♦ Pattern

Abstract:

$$\frac{2}{5} + \frac{3}{10}$$

$$\frac{4}{10} + \frac{3}{10} = \frac{7}{10}$$

Figure 7.3 Differentiation

3 Differentiated Lessons		
In this series of lessons, students are working on adding fractions. They are developing this concept through concrete activities, pictorial activities and abstract activities. Here are some things to think about as you do these lessons.		
Emerging	**On Grade Level**	**Above Grade Level**
Do a lot of work with students looking at fraction strips and where the fractions are on the number line. Be sure to review adding fractions with like denominators.	Do a lot of work with different manipulatives. Students should use pattern blocks, fraction strips, fraction squares, number lines and other tools. Students should do a lot of work where they not only have to solve but also have to tell fraction addition word problems. Be sure to work with mixed numbers.	Think about opportunities for enrichment. In what ways can you get students to do projects where they are working on this math with real-life situations? What types of math projects can they do where they are taking their learning further being curious, wondering about the world they live in and using critical thinking skills?

 Looking for Misunderstandings and Common Errors

This is a tricky skill for many students. The way they learn is to work with fraction manipulatives to find common denominators. Students will often just add the numerators and add the denominators without finding a common denominator. It will look like this: 3/4 + 2/3 = 5/7.

Figure 7.4 Anchor Chart

Fraction Strips

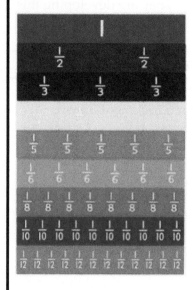

Fraction Strip Template

Pictorial:

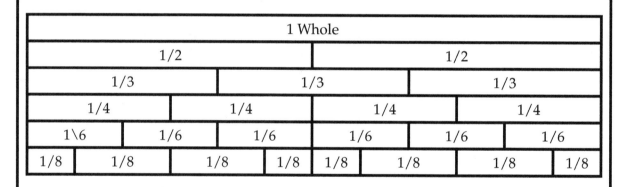

1 Whole							
1/2				1/2			
1/3			1/3		1/3		
1/4		1/4		1/4		1/4	
1\6		1/6	1/6	1/6		1/6	1/6
1/8	1/8	1/8	1/8	1/8	1/8	1/8	1/8

Abstract

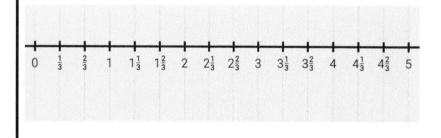

Figure 7.5 Concrete Introduction

Introduction to Concrete Explorations

Launch	**Teacher:** Today we are going to work on adding fractions with pattern blocks. **Vocabulary:** halves, thirds, fourths, fifths, sixths, eighths, tenths, twelfths, denominator, numerator, whole number, sum, addends **Math Talk:** I added ___ and ___. My sum is ___.
Model	**Teacher:** Everyone has a baggie with pattern blocks. We are going to practice adding fractions with pattern blocks. Let's look at 1/3 + 1/2. Do it and then be ready to explain your thinking. **Trini:** I had to find a common denominator. I changed both of them to sixths. I got 2/6 and 3/6. I got 5/6. 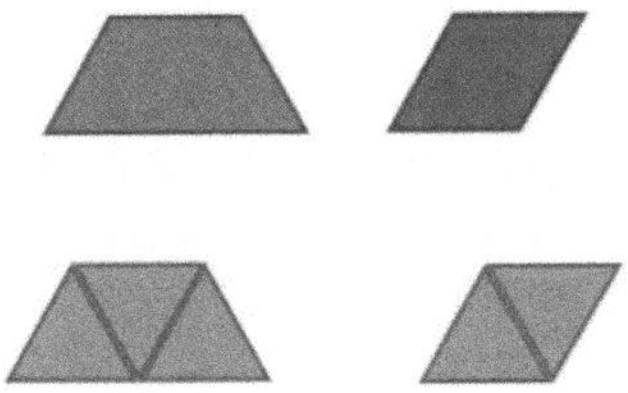
Checking for Understanding	**Teacher:** Let's add 2/6 + 1/3. (Everyone models this, and they discuss the model). I am going to give each one of you sets of problems to explore. Then, we will go around, and each of you will pick a problem to share. **Mary:** I had to find a common denominator. I changed both of them to sixths. I got 2/6 and 2/6. I got 4/6. 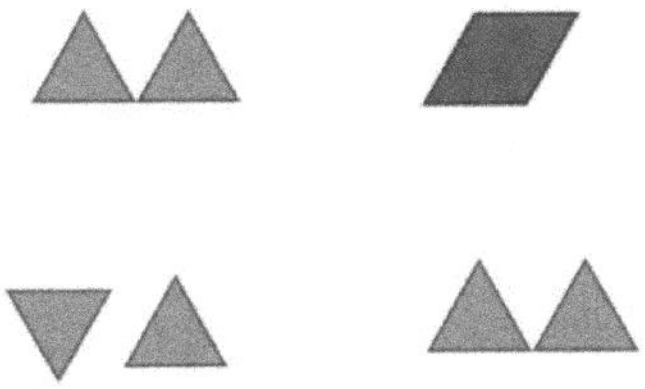

Figure 7.6 Concrete Student Activity

	Concrete Student Activity
Guided Practice/ Checking for Understanding	**Teacher:** Who wants to go next? **Maria:** I had 1/2 + 3/4. I had to find a common denominator. I used fourths. I added 2/4 and 3/4. I got 5/4, which is 1 and a 1/4. 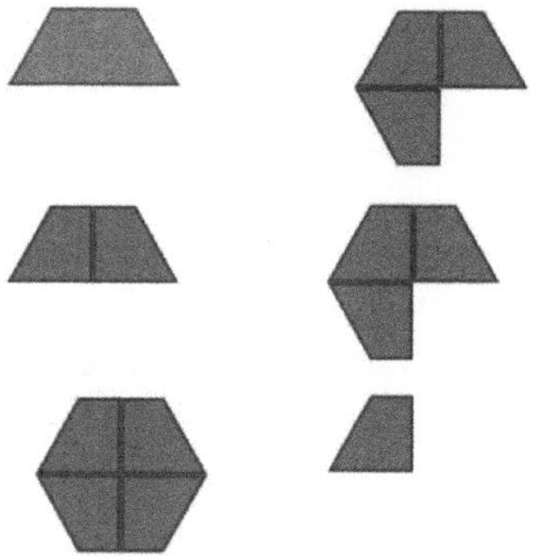
Set Up for Independent Practice	Every child gets to share their thinking about decomposing a fraction and how they reasoned about it. We are going to be talking more about this in the upcoming days. Are there any questions? What was interesting today? What was tricky?

Figure 7.7 Lesson Close

Close
◆ What did we do today? ◆ What was the math we were practicing? ◆ What were we doing with our pattern blocks? ◆ Was this easy or tricky? ◆ Are there any questions?

Figure 7.8 Visual Introduction

	Introduction to Visual Explorations:
Launch	**Teacher:** Today we are going to work on adding fractions with sketches. **Vocabulary:** halves, thirds, fourths, fifths, sixths, eighths, tenths, twelfths, denominator, numerator, whole number, sum, addends **Math Talk:** I added ___ and ___. My sum is ____.
Model	**Teacher:** Everyone has a baggie with pattern block paper and pattern block pieces. We are going to practice adding fractions with these tools. Let's add 3/6 and 1/2. Who can explain this model? **Maria:** I can. I changed everything to sixths. I got 3/6 plus 3/6, and I got 6 sixths, which is equivalent to 1 whole.

Introduction to Visual Explorations:

Checking for Understanding	**Teacher:** Let's add 2/3 and 2/6. (Everyone models this, and they discuss the model). I am going to give each one of you sets of problems to explore. Then, we will go around, and each of you will pick a problem to share.

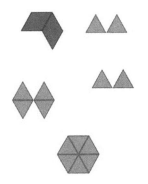

Terri:
I changed everything to sixths, and I got 4/6 and 2/6, which is 6/6, which is 1 whole.

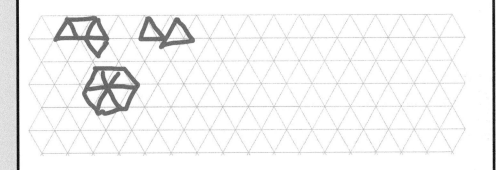

Figure 7.9 Visual Student Activity

Visual Student Activity

Guided Practice/ Checking for Understanding	**Teacher:** Marcos, explain what you did to solve your problem. **Marcos:** I pulled 1/6 and 1/3. So I changed the thirds to sixths and added 1/6 and 2/6, and I got 3/6, which is 1/2. 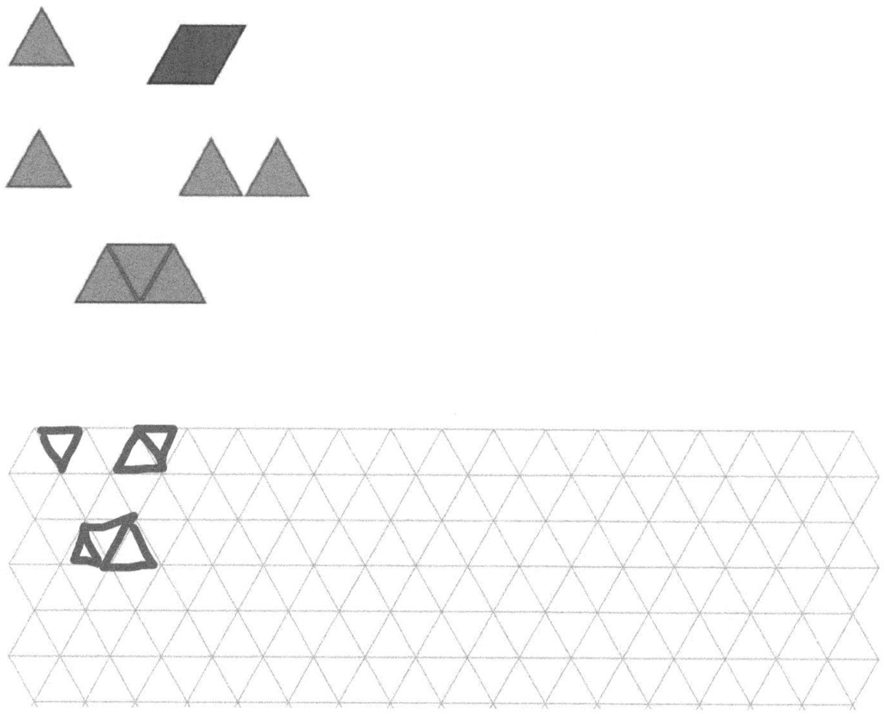
Set Up for Independent Practice	Teacher gives everybody a chance to do and discuss a problem. After everyone has shared, the lesson ends. We are going to be talking more about this in the upcoming days. Are there any questions? What was interesting today? What was tricky?

Figure 7.10 Lesson Close

Close
◆ What did we do today? ◆ What was the math we were practicing? ◆ What were we doing with our sketches? ◆ Was this easy or tricky? ◆ Are there any questions?

Figure 7.11 Pattern Block Paper

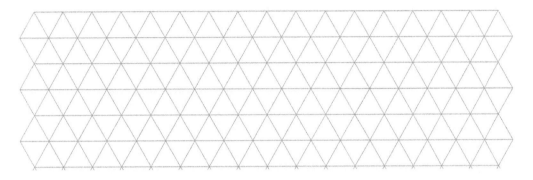

Figure 7.12 Abstract Introduction

Introduction to Abstract Explorations

Launch	**Teacher:** Today we are going to work on adding fractions on a number line. **Vocabulary:** thirds, halves, sixths, fourths, eighths, tenths, twelfths, whole number, sum, addends **Math Talk:** I added ___ and ___. My sum is ____.
Model	**Teacher:** Let's look at adding 1/3 and 2/6. Here are some number lines. Now, what is a common denominator for these two fractions? **Kayla:** Sixths. 1/3 is 2/6, and we already have another 2/6. **Teacher:** Okay, so we are going to make this number line sixths. **Tim:** We can jump 2/6 plus 1/6 plus 1/6, and we get 4/6. 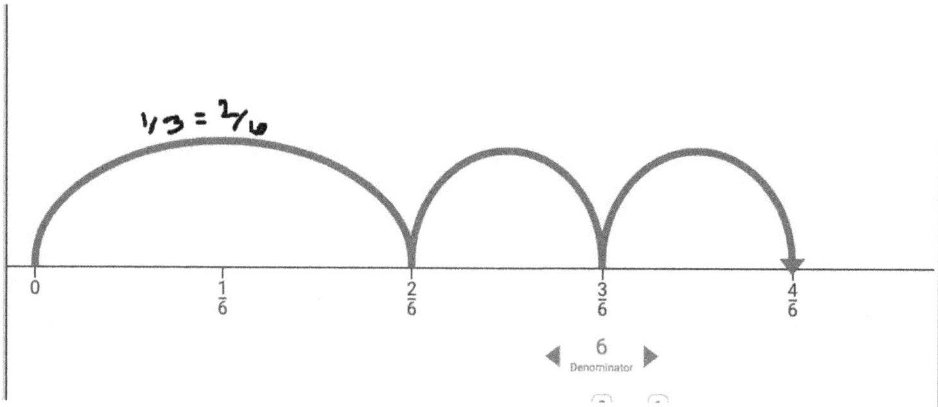 $1/3 = 2/6$ 0 $\frac{1}{6}$ $\frac{2}{6}$ $\frac{3}{6}$ $\frac{4}{6}$ ◀ 6 ▶ Denominator
Checking for Understanding	**Teacher:** Okay, let's try another one. 1/5 and 2/10. What should we do? **Maria:** Make it tenths because that is a common denominator. **Joey:** Then jump 2/10. **Tami:** 1/5 is 2/10, so we jump 2/10 more, and we get 4/10.

Figure 7.13 Abstract Student Activity

	Abstract Student Activity
Guided Practice/ Checking for Understanding	**Teacher:** I am going to give each one of you a number line templates and some problems. You are going to solve them and share your thinking with a buddy, and then be ready to share with the group. **Teacher:** Katie, tell me what you are doing. **Katie:** The problem is 2/3 + 4/12. I made the number line twelfths, and then I jumped 4/12, and then I jumped 8/12, and I got 12/12, which is 1 whole. 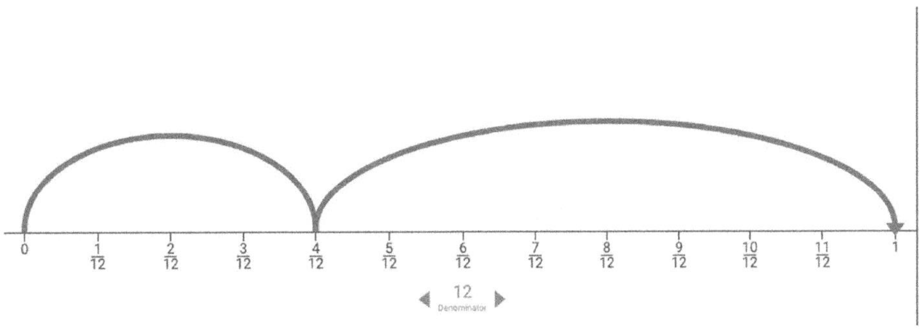
Set Up for Independent Practice	**Teacher:** Okay, turn and tell your neighbor what you are thinking about what we have learned today. If you want to stay behind and practice a bit more you can; otherwise, you can go to your workstations.

Figure 7.14 Lesson Close

Close
◆ What did we do today?
◆ What was the math we were practicing?
◆ What were we doing with our number line templates?
◆ Was this easy or tricky?
◆ Are there any questions?

Section Summary

Adding fractions with unlike denominators is tricky. Students have to really understand what it means to find a common denominator. I like to start with pattern blocks and fraction tiles to teach students how to find a common denominator. Take the time to teach the concept with hands-on activities and the students will remember it because they have done it. It is one thing to try to remember a random rule, and it is another to do math with understanding. Make sure that students can model their thinking in more than one way and that they can explain the expressions.

Subtracting Fractions

Figure 7.15 Overview

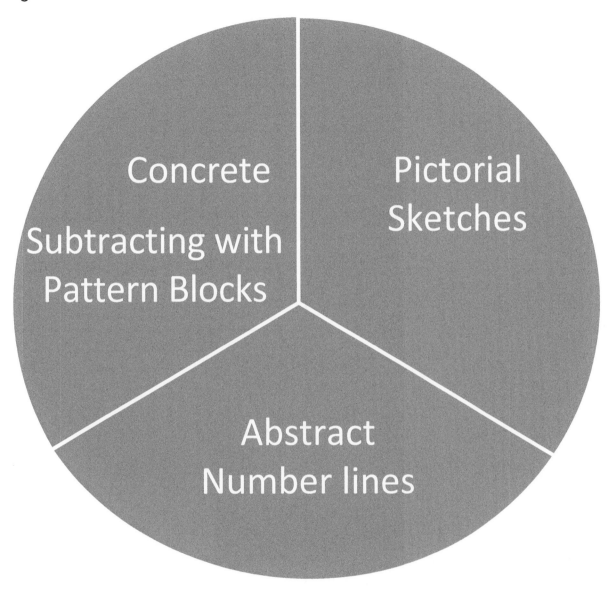

Figure 7.16 Planning Template

Subtracting Fractions With Unlike Denominators	
Big Idea: Numbers; Operation Meaning and Relationships **Enduring Understanding:** Students will understand how to subtract fractions with unlike denominators. **Essential Question:** Why are fractions important? How do we use them in real life? **I can statement:** I can discuss and model subtracting fractions with unlike denominators.	**Materials** ♦ Tools: Fraction Strips ♦ Templates: Fraction Strip Template ♦ Crayons ♦ Paper
Cycle of Engagement **Concrete:**   **Pictorial:** $\frac{3}{6} - \frac{1}{6} = \frac{2}{6}$  **Abstract:** 1/2 − 1/6 = 3/6 − 1/6 = 2/6	**Vocabulary & Language Frames** **Vocabulary:** whole, halves, thirds, fourths, sixths, eighths, numerator, denominator, sum, addends, **Math Processes/Practices** ♦ Problem-Solving ♦ Reasoning ♦ Models ♦ Tools ♦ Precision ♦ Structure ♦ Pattern

Figure 7.17 Differentiation

3 Differentiated Lessons
In this series of lessons, students are working on the concept of subtracting fractions with unlike denominators. They are developing this concept through concrete activities, pictorial activities and abstract activities. Here are some things to think about as you do these lessons.

Emerging	On Grade Level	Above Grade Level
Students should first review work with manipulatives to subtract fractions with like denominators.	Students work with manipulatives to find common denominators and to make sense of the algorithm. Students are also subtracting mixed numbers.	Think about opportunities for enrichment. In what ways can you get students to do projects where they are working on this math with real-life situations. What types of math projects can they do where they are taking their learning further being curious, wondering about the world they live in and using critical thinking skills?

 Looking for Misunderstandings and Common Errors

Students should do a great deal of work with manipulatives so they understand what they are doing. They should be making a great deal of connections with the concrete manipulatives, sketches and the algorithm. Don't rush to the algorithm because often students learn to do it without understanding. Students will make mistakes like subtracting both the numerator and the denominator. For example, students will solve 3/4 – 1/2 = 2/2.

Figure 7.18 Anchor Chart

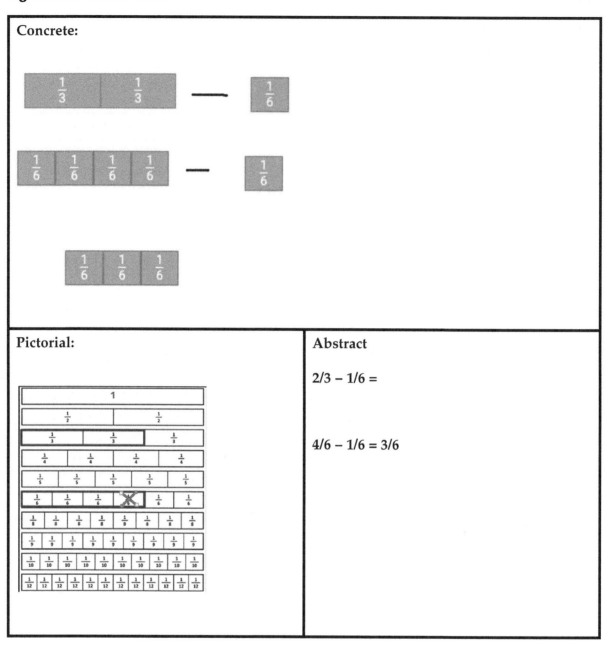

Figure 7.19 Concrete Introduction

Introduction to Concrete Explorations

Launch	**Teacher:** Today we are going to work on subtracting fractions with pattern blocks.
	Vocabulary: halves, thirds, fourths, fifths, sixths, eighths, tenths, twelfths, denominator, numerator, whole number, difference,
	Math Talk: I subtracted ___ and ___. My difference is ____.
Model	**Teacher:** Everyone has a baggie with pattern blocks. We are going to practice subtracting fractions with pattern blocks and drawings. Let's look at 2/3 – 1/6. Do it and then be ready to explain your thinking. **Trini:** I had to find a common denominator. I changed both of them to sixths. I subtracted 1/6 from 4/6. I have 3/6 left.
Checking for Understanding	**Teacher:** Let's subtract 5/6 – 1/3. (Everyone models this, and they discuss the model.) I am going to give each one of you sets of problems to explore. Then, we will go around, and each of you will pick a problem to share. **Carl:** I made everything into sixths . . . so the third became 2/6 and 5/6 take away 2/6 is 3/6.

Figure 7.20 Concrete Student Activity

	Concrete Student Activities
Guided Practice/ Checking for Understanding	**Teacher:** Mary, what did you do? **Mary:** I had 1 – 2/3. I had to find a common denominator. I changed both of them to thirds. I had 3/3 minus 2/3. I had 1/3 left.
Set Up for Independent Practice	**Teacher:** Okay, turn and tell your neighbor what you are thinking about what we have learned today. What does it mean to find a common denominator? **Kylie:** It means all the pieces have to be the same. If you want to stay behind and practice a bit more you can; otherwise, you can go to your workstations.

Figure 7.21 Lesson Close

Close
♦ What did we do today?   ♦ What was the math we were practicing?   ♦ What were we doing with our pattern blocks?   ♦ Was this easy or tricky?   ♦ Are there any questions?

Figure 7.22 Visual Introduction

Introduction to a Visual Explorations

Launch	**Teacher:** Today we are going to work on subtracting fractions with sketches. **Vocabulary:** halves, thirds, fourths, fifths, sixths, eighths, tenths, twelfths, denominator, numerator, whole number, difference, **Math Talk:** I subtracted ___ and ___. My difference is ___.
Model	**Teacher:** Everyone has a baggie with paper fraction pieces. We are going to practice subtracting fractions with these tools. Let's subtract 3/6 from 1/2. Who can explain this model?

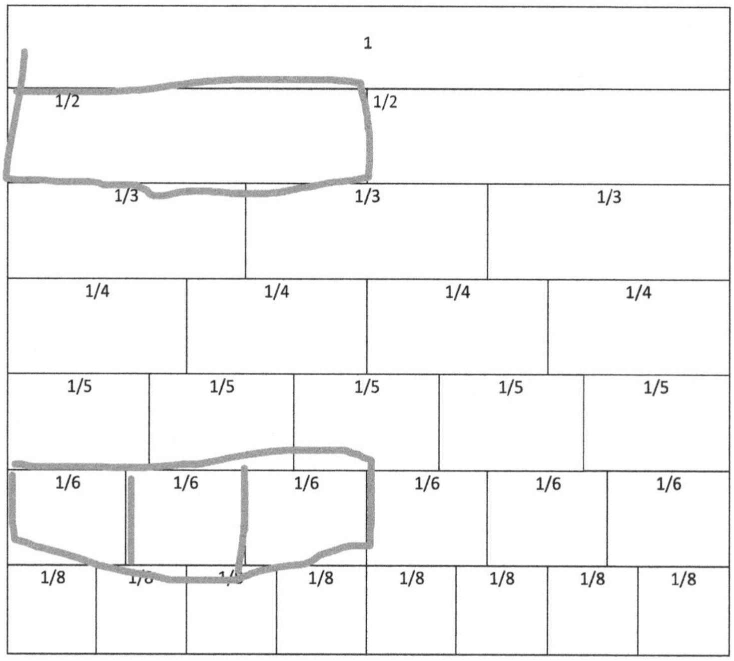

Maria: I did. I changed everything to sixths. 1/2 equals 3/6. I got 3/6 minus 3/6, and I got 0 sixths.

Introduction to a Visual Explorations

Checking for Understanding

Teacher: Let's subtract 1/4 from 1. (Everyone models this, and they discuss the model).

Elena: Well we make everything be partitioned into the same parts. I got 4/4 – 1/4 is 3/4.

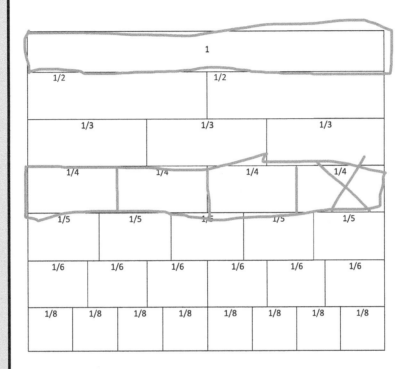

I am going to give each one of you sets of problems to explore. Then, we will go around, and each of you will pick a problem to share.

Figure 7.23 Visual Student Activity

<center>**Visual Student Activity**</center>	
Guided Practice/ Checking for Understanding	**Teacher:** Marcos, explain what you did to solve your problem. **Marcos:** I pulled 1/6 from 2/3. So I changed the thirds to sixths, and I had 4/6. I subtracted 1/6 from it, and I got 3/6. 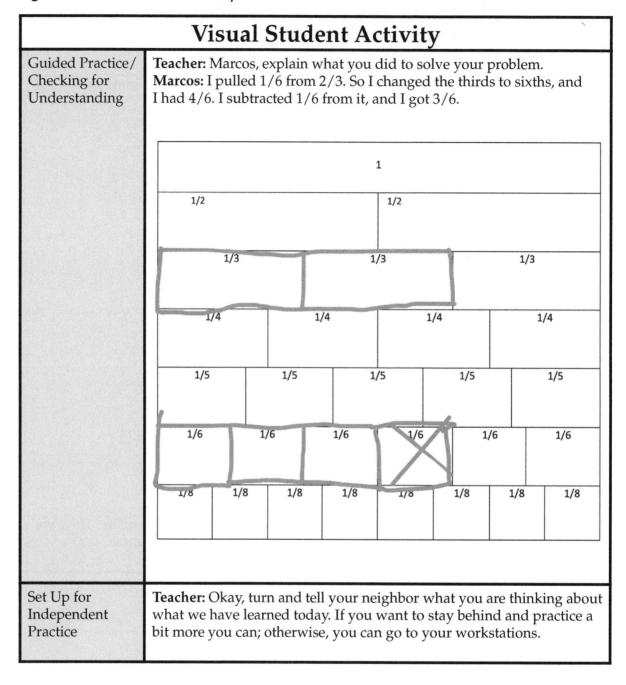
Set Up for Independent Practice	**Teacher:** Okay, turn and tell your neighbor what you are thinking about what we have learned today. If you want to stay behind and practice a bit more you can; otherwise, you can go to your workstations.

Figure 7.24 Lesson Close

Close
♦ What did we do today?
♦ What was the math we were practicing?
♦ What were we doing with our sketches?
♦ Was this easy or tricky?
♦ Are there any questions?

Figure 7.25 Fraction Strip Template

1							
1/2				1/2			
1/3		1/3			1/3		
1/4		¼		1/4		1/4	
1/5		1/5		1/5		1/5	1/5
1/6	1/6		1/6		1/6	1/6	1/6
1/8	1/8	1/8	1/8	1/8	1/8	1/8	1/8

Figure 7.26 Abstract Introduction

	Introduction to Abstract Lesson
Launch	**Teacher:** Today we are going to work on subtracting fractions on a number line. **Vocabulary:** decimals, tenths, hundredths, thousands, whole number, difference **Math Talk:** I subtracted ___ and ___. My difference is ____.
Model	**Teacher:** Let's look at subtracting 1/3 from 4/6. Here is a number line. Now, what is a common denominator for these two fractions. **Kim:** Sixths **Teacher:** Okay, so we are going to make this number line sixths. First let's find 4/6. And then what next? **Todd:** 1/3 is 2/6, so we should jump back 2/6. We get 2/6.
Checking for Understanding	**Teacher:** Okay, let's try another one. 4/5 and 2/10. What should we do? **Marta:** Make it tenths because that is a common denominator. **Joe:** 4/5 is 8/10. So we start at 8/10 and subtract 2/10. **Tami:** We get 6/10. **Teacher:** I am going to give each one of you number line templates and some problems. You are going to solve them and share your thinking with a buddy, and then be ready to share with the group.

Figure 7.27 Abstract Student Activity

<table>
<tr><td colspan="2" style="text-align:center">Abstract Student Activity</td></tr>
<tr>
<td>Guided Practice/ Checking for Understanding</td>
<td>

Teacher: Katya, tell me what you are doing.

Katya The problem is 2/3 – 1/12. I made the number line twelfths, and then I started on 8/12, and I jumped back 1/12. I got 7/12.

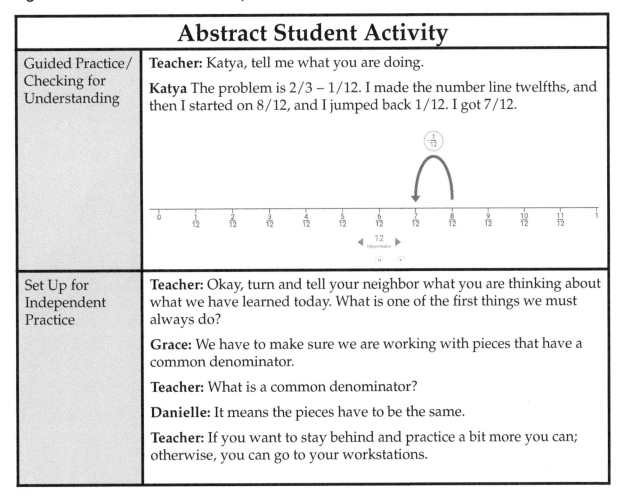

</td>
</tr>
<tr>
<td>Set Up for Independent Practice</td>
<td>

Teacher: Okay, turn and tell your neighbor what you are thinking about what we have learned today. What is one of the first things we must always do?

Grace: We have to make sure we are working with pieces that have a common denominator.

Teacher: What is a common denominator?

Danielle: It means the pieces have to be the same.

Teacher: If you want to stay behind and practice a bit more you can; otherwise, you can go to your workstations.

</td>
</tr>
</table>

Figure 7.28 Lesson Close

<table>
<tr><td style="text-align:center">Close</td></tr>
<tr><td>

♦ What did we do today?
♦ What was the math we were practicing?
♦ What were we doing with our number lines?
♦ Was this easy or tricky?
♦ Are there any questions?

</td></tr>
</table>

Section Summary

Subtracting fractions needs to be taught with different models such as fraction strips, squares and circles. After students do a great deal of work with the concrete manipulatives, then they should do work with the templates of these manipulatives. When students can model their thinking with concrete and paper manipulatives as well as sketch out their thinking, then start playing games in which they have to just subtract the fractions with no scaffolds.

Figure 7.29 Overview

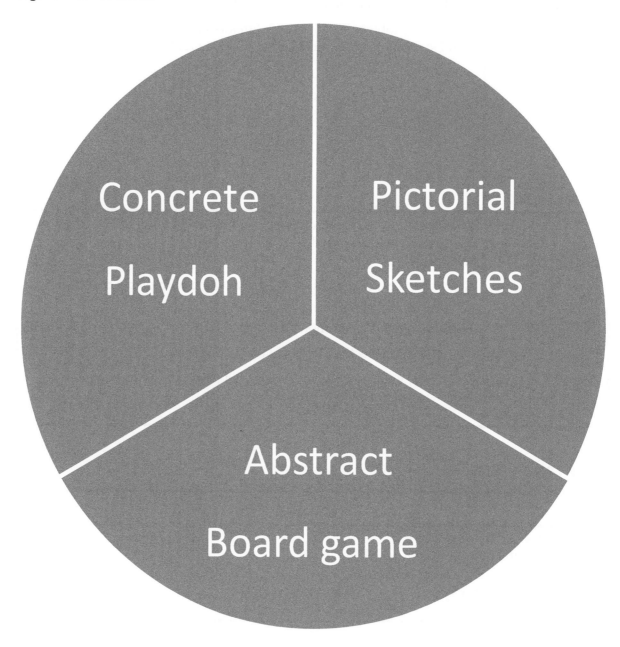

Figure 7.30 Planning Template

Multiplying Fractions

Big Idea: Numbers; Operation Meaning and Relationships. **Enduring Understanding:** Students will understand how to multiply fractions. **Essential Question:** Why are fractions important? How do we use them in real life? **I can statement:** I can discuss and model multiplying fractions.	**Materials** ♦ Tools: Fraction Strips ♦ Templates: Fraction Strip Template ♦ Crayons ♦ Paper

Cycle of Engagement **Concrete:** ½ x ½ = ¼ 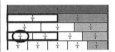 **Pictorial:** ½ of ½ 	**Vocabulary & Language Frames** **Vocabulary:** whole, halves, thirds, fourths, sixths, eighths, numerator, denominator, sum, addends, **Math Talk:** I multiplied ___ and ___. The product is ___.

1 Whole			
1/2		1/2	
1/3	1/3		1/3
1/4	1/4	1/4	1/4

Abstract:
$1/2 \times 1/2 = 1/4$

Math Processes/Practices
♦ **Problem-Solving**
♦ **Reasoning**
♦ **Models**
♦ **Tools**
♦ **Precision**
♦ **Structure**
♦ **Pattern**

Figure 7.31 Differentiation

3 Differentiated Lessons
In this series of lessons, students are working on understanding multiplying fractions. They are developing this concept through concrete activities, pictorial activities and abstract activities. Here are some things to think about as you do these lessons.

Emerging	On Grade Level	Above Grade Level
Students should work with different models, including fraction circles, squares and strips. Be sure to review multiplying a whole number by a fraction.	Students should use models to understand how to multiply fractions. There should be a focus on having students explain what the concept is and what it means to do it. Students should be able to not only solve stories but also tell them about the multiplication of fractions.	Think about opportunities for enrichment. In what ways can you get students to do projects where they are working on this math with real-life situations? What types of math projects can they do where they are taking their learning further being curious, wondering about the world they live in and using critical thinking skills?

 # Looking for Misunderstandings and Common Errors

Students usually have trouble explaining the concept, but they understand the procedure. Do a lot of storytelling in which they have to give a story about a multiplication expression. Sometimes students will keep a common denominator and multiply the numerator. For example, they will solve this way: 3/5 × 4/5 = 12/5. Other times they will multiply the whole number and then the fractions. For example they will solve: 2 1/4 x 3 1/2 = 6 1/8 (NCTM, session 10319).

Figure 7.32 Anchor Chart

Multiplying Fractions

When we are multiplying fractions, we are talking about a piece of a piece. So, 1/2 times 1/2 is really a 1/2 of a 1/2.

Concrete

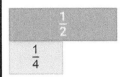

Pictorial

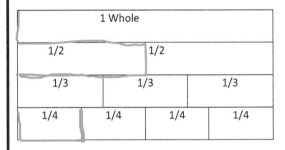

Abstract
- ◆ $1/2 \times 1/2$
- ◆ 1/2 of a 1/2
- ◆ $1/2 \times 1/2 = 1/4$

Figure 7.33 Concrete Introduction

	Introduction to Concrete Explorations
Launch	**Teacher:** Today we are going to work on multiplying fractions **Vocabulary:** halves, thirds, fourths, fifths, sixths, eighths, tenths, twelfths, denominator, numerator, whole number, factors, product **Math Talk:** I multiplied ___ and ___. The product is ____.
Model	**Teacher:** Listen. I am going to tell you a story. I had a great uncle named Nunck. He was my grandfather's brother. He loved gum. He always had gum. If we asked him for gum, he would take out a piece and break some off and tell us to share it. So if he gave me 1/2 of a piece, and then I had to give my brother half of my half . . . how much would my brother get? Let's explore: **Here is the piece of gum. Here is half of it. Here is half of the half: 1/2 times 1/2 is 1/4:**
Checking for Understanding	**Teacher:** Let's try another one. What if my Great Uncle gave me a 1/3 of a piece of his gum. I gave my brother 1/2 of my 1/3. How much would my brother get? **Here is the piece of gum. Here is 1/3 of it. Here is half of the 1/3: 1/2 times 1/3 is 1/6:**

Figure 7.34 Concrete Student Activity

Concrete Student Activity	
Guided Practice/Checking for Understanding	**Teacher:** Let's try another one. What if my great uncle gave me a 1/4 of a piece of his gum. I gave my brother 1/2 of my 1/4. How much would my brother get? Let's model it. Who wants to explain? **Mikey:** Here is the whole piece. Here is ¼ of it. Here is ½ of the ¼. ½ times ¼ is ⅛ ½ × ¼ = ⅛. It is a piece of a piece. 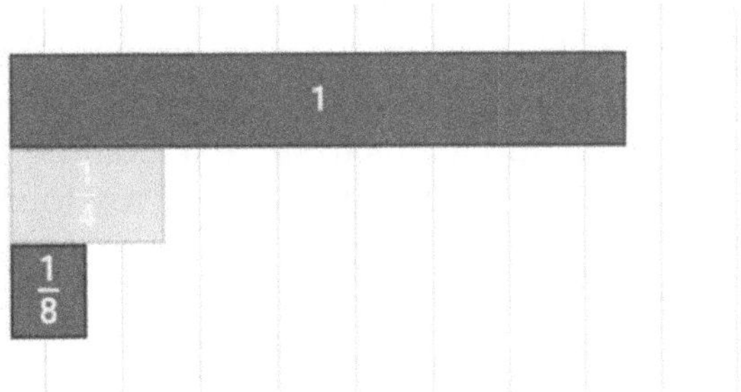
Set Up for Independent Practice	**Teacher:** Okay, turn and tell your neighbor what you are thinking about what we have learned today. If you want to stay behind and practice a bit more you can; otherwise, you can go to your workstations.

Figure 7.35 Lesson Close

Close
◆ What did we do today? ◆ What was the math we were practicing? ◆ What were we doing with our fraction tiles? ◆ Was this easy or tricky? ◆ Are there any questions?

Figure 7.36 Visual Introduction

Introduction to Visual Explorations

Launch	**Teacher:** Today we are going to work on multiplying fractions with sketches. **Vocabulary:** halves, thirds, fourths, fifths, sixths, eighths, tenths, twelfths, denominator, numerator, whole number, factors, product **Math Talk:** I multiplied ___ and ___. The product is ___.
Model	**Teacher:** Listen I am going to tell you a story. I had a great uncle named Nunck. He was my grandfather's brother. He loved gum. He always had gum. If we asked him for gum, he would take out a piece and break some off and tell us to share it. So if he gave me 1/4 of a piece, and then I had to give my brother half of my fourth . . . how much would my brother get? **Let's explore:** 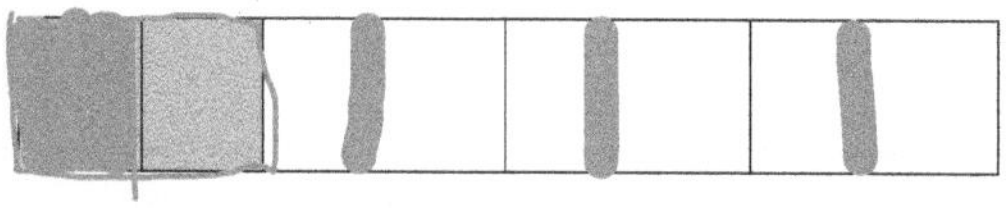 **Taylor:** So my brother actually got 1/8 of the gum. 1/2 of a fourth is 1/8. I split my piece in half, and then I split the other pieces in half as well, and I got 8 pieces, and my brother got 1 of those 8 pieces. He got a piece of a piece.
Checking for Understanding	**Teacher:** Let's try another one. What if my great uncle gave me a 1/3 of a piece of his gum. I gave my brother 1/3 of my 1/3. How much would my brother get? Let's Explore: 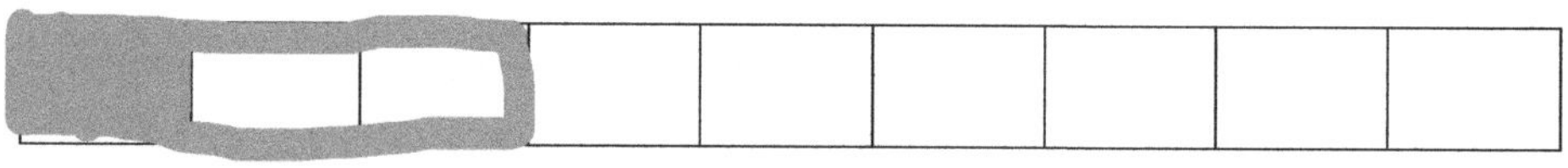 **Todd:** So I got a third of the gum. I cut my thirds into thirds. So my brother got 1/9 of the piece of gum. He got a piece of my piece.

Figure 7.37 Visual Student Activity

	Visual Student Activity
Guided Practice/Checking for Unerstanding	**Teacher:** Let's try another one. What if my great uncle gave me a 1/2 of a piece of his gum. I gave my brother 1/2 of my 1/2. How much would my brother get? Let's explore? 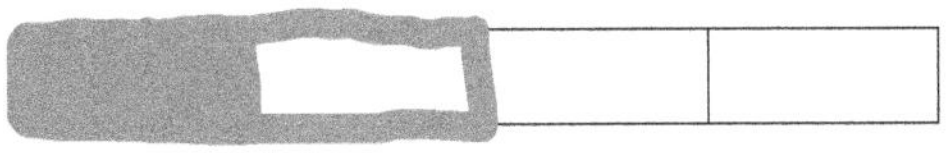 **Jacob:** He would get 1/4 because 1/2 of a 1/2 is 1/4. See here is my model.
Set Up for Independent Practice	**Teacher:** Okay, turn and tell your neighbor what you are thinking about what we have learned today. If you want to stay behind and practice a bit more you can; otherwise, you can go to your workstations..

Figure 7.38 Lesson Close

Close
♦ What did we do today?   ♦ What was the math we were practicing?   ♦ What were we doing with our sketches?   ♦ Was this easy or tricky?   ♦ Are there any questions?

Figure 7.39 Abstract Introduction

Introduction to Abstract Explorations

| Launch | **Teacher:** Today we are going to work on multiplying fractions with a board game.
Vocabulary: halves, thirds, fourths, fifths, sixths, eighths, tenths, twelfths, denominator, numerator, whole number, factors, product
Math Talk:
I multiplied ___ and ___. The product is ____.

Multiplying Fractions
Instructions: Spin the spinner. Whoever has the lowest number goes first. Move that many spaces and solve the problem where you land. The first person to land on finish wins. 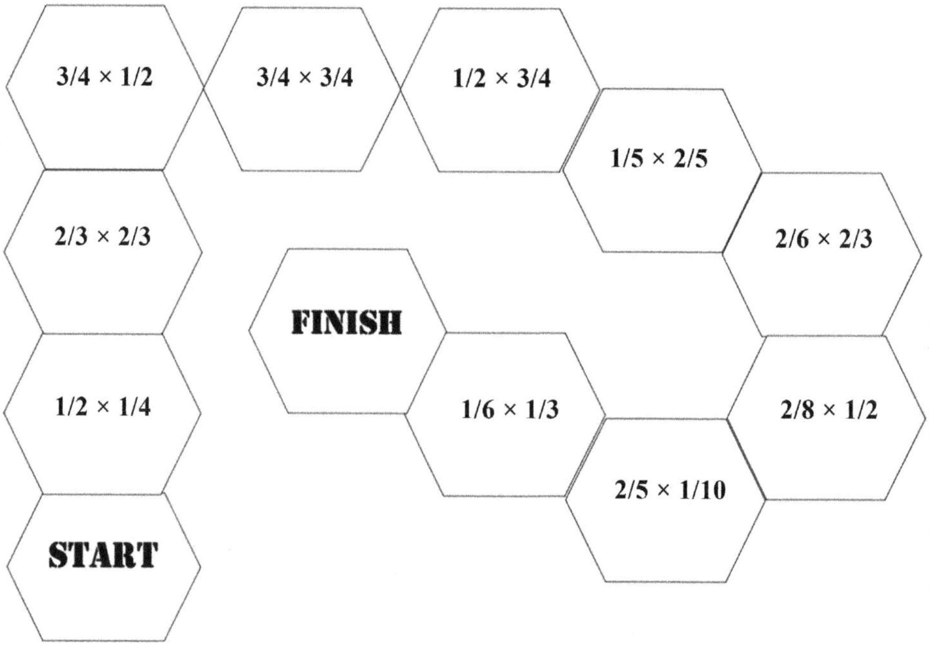 

3/4 × 1/2   3/4 × 3/4   1/2 × 3/4
1/5 × 2/5
2/3 × 2/3   2/6 × 2/3
FINISH
1/2 × 1/4   1/6 × 1/3   2/8 × 1/2
2/5 × 1/10
START

1 2 3 |

Introduction to Abstract Explorations

Model	**Teacher:** Here is the board game. The problems on it are multiplication problems. You spin, land on a problem and solve it. If you are correct, you stay there. If you are incorrect, you have to go back a space. Whoever reaches finish first wins. Are there any questions about how to play? Also, who can explain the procedure for multiplying fractions? **Mario:** I can. You multiply the numerators and the denominators.
Checking for Understanding	**Teacher:** Who can explain the concept? What are we doing when we are multiplying fractions? **Marta:** We are looking for a piece of a piece . . . like with the gum stories. **Teacher:** So, if I landed on $2/6 \times 1/3$ what would the answer be? **Tom:** The answer would be 2/18. **Teacher:** Who agrees? (All the students nod their heads in agreement).

Figure 7.40 Abstract Student Activity

Abstract Student Activities

Guided Practice/ Checking for Understanding	**Teacher:** You all are going to play the game in groups of 2s or 3s. I am going to watch, take some notes and ask you some questions. **Teacher:** Kelli and Mike, tell me about a problem that each of you solved so far. **Katie:** The problem I solved is $2/3 \times 1/4$. I got 2/12. **Mike:** The problem I solved is $1/4 \times 1/4$, and I got 1/16.
Set Up for Independent Practice	**Teacher:** Okay, as we end the session, turn and tell your neighbor what you are thinking about what we have practiced today. If you want to stay behind and practice a bit more you can; otherwise, you can go to your workstations.

Figure 7.41 Lesson Close

Close
◆ What did we do today? ◆ What was the math we were practicing? ◆ What were we doing with our board game? ◆ Was this easy or tricky? ◆ Are there any questions?

Section Summary

Multiplying fractions is an easy procedure. Students have to really understand what it means. I often use playdough and have the students act it out through storytelling. Take the time to teach the concept with hands-on activities and the students will remember it because they have done it. It is one thing to try to remember a random rule, and it is another to do math with understanding. Make sure that students can model their thinking in more than one way and that they can explain the expressions.

Figure 7.42 Multiplying Fraction Games

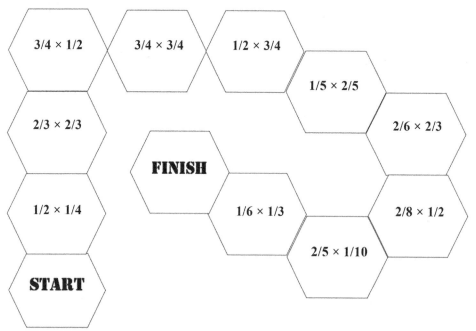

Multiplying Fractions

Instructions: Spin the spinner. Whoever has the lowest number goes first. Move that many spaces and solve the problem where you land. The first person to land on finish wins.

3/4 × 1/2

3/4 × 3/4

1/2 × 3/4

1/5 × 2/5

2/6 × 2/3

2/3 × 2/3

FINISH

1/2 × 1/4

1/6 × 1/3

2/8 × 1/2

2/5 × 1/10

START

Dividing Fractions

Figure 7.43 Overview

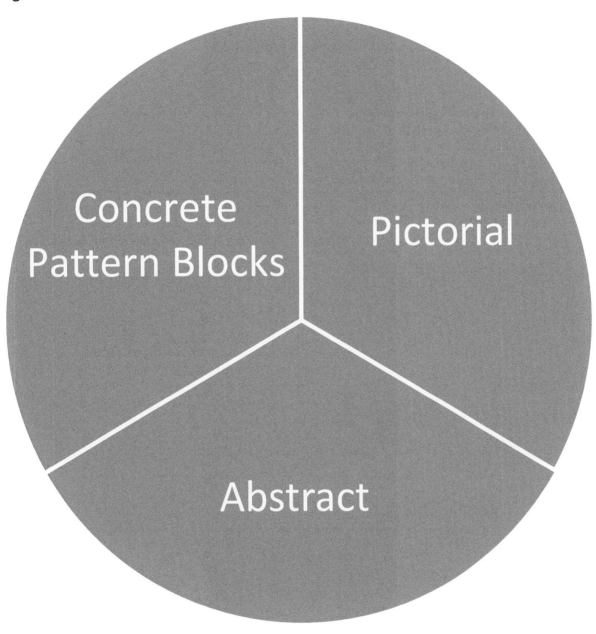

Figure 7.44 Planning Template

Dividing Fractions

Big Idea: Numbers; Operation Meaning and Relationships **Enduring Understanding:** Students will understand how to divide fractions with whole numbers. **Essential Question:** Why are fractions important? How do we use them in real life? **I can statement:** I can discuss and model dividing fractions and whole numbers.	**Materials** ♦ Tools: Fraction Strips ♦ Templates: Fraction Strip Template ♦ Crayons ♦ Paper

Cycle of Engagement Concrete: $1 \div 1/5 = 5$ 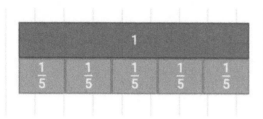 Pictorial: $2 \div 1/6 = 12$  Abstract: $3 \div 1/3 = 9$	**Vocabulary & Language Frames** **Vocabulary:** whole, halves, thirds, fourths, sixths, eighths, numerator, denominator, quotient, divisor, dividend **Math Talk:** I divided ___ by ___. The quotient is ___. **Math Processes/Practices** ♦ Problem-Solving ♦ Reasoning ♦ Models ♦ Tools ♦ Precision ♦ Structure ♦ Pattern

Figure 7.45 Differentiation

3 Differentiated Lessons
In this series of lessons, students are working on understanding dividing fractions and whole numbers. They are developing this concept through concrete activities, pictorial activities and abstract activities. Here are some things to think about as you do these lessons.

Emerging	On Grade Level	Above Grade Level
Students should work with different models, including fraction circles, squares and strips. They should tell many stories about dividing a fraction by a whole number and a whole number by a fraction.	Students should be able to solve problems and tell problems. You can really tell if they understand when they can tell you a problem about an expression.	Make sure that you have students work on and find when and where we would need to do this in real life. You will do this with all students; however, with students working above grade level, you could do a more extensive project.

 Looking for Misunderstandings and Common Errors

Students have trouble explaining dividing a fraction by a whole number. They get mixed up on the procedure. Have them tell and illustrate division stories. Students will make various errors. One common error is that students will think that division is just like addition of fractions and they will work on getting a common denominator. For example $6 \div 2/3 = 6/1 \times 2/3 = 18/3 \times 2/3 = 36/3 = 12$ (cited in Maelasari, 2017). Another error that students make when dividing fractions is that they think dividing by 1/2 is the same as dividing in half. For example, students will divide $6 \div 1/2 = 3$.

Figure 7.46 Anchor Chart

Concrete: 1 ÷ 1/5 = 5

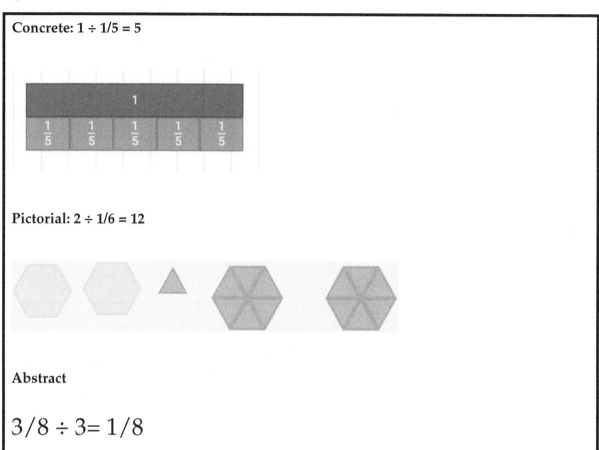

Pictorial: 2 ÷ 1/6 = 12

Abstract

3/8 ÷ 3= 1/8

Figure 7.47 Concrete Introduction

	Introduction to Concrete Explorations	
Launch	**Teacher:** Today we are going to work on dividing fractions with pattern blocks **Vocabulary:** halves, thirds, fourths, fifths, sixths, eighths, tenths, twelfths, denominator, numerator, whole number, dividend, divisor, quotient **Math Talk:** I divided ___ by ___. The quotient is ____.	
Model	**Teacher:** Listen I am going to tell you a story. Grandma Betsy made a cake. She cut it into thirds. How many pieces did she get? **Let's explore:** **Here is the cake:** **Here is 1/3.** **How many of these can we take out of this?** **Taylor:** 3/3 makes 1 whole.	
Checking for Understanding	**Teacher:** Listen, I am going to tell you a story. Grandma Betsy made 2 cakes. She cut them into sixths. How many pieces did she get? **Let's explore:** **Here are the cakes:** **Here is 1/6.** **How many of these can we take out of this?** 	

Figure 7.48 Concrete Student Activity

	Concrete Student Activity
Guided Practice/Checking for Understanding	**Michael:** She got 6 pieces out of each cake. So if she had 2 cakes, she got 12 pieces. **Teacher:** Okay, you are going to each work on a problem and model it. You will share your work with your buddy, and then be ready to come back to the group and share with us all. **Teacher:** Michelle, tell me what you are doing? **Michelle:** I had 2 cakes divided by 1/4. I know that 4/4 makes 1 whole, with 4 pieces. So 2 cakes make 8 pieces. So 2 divided by 1/4 is 8. 
Set Up for Independent Practice	**Teacher:** Okay, turn and tell your neighbor what you are thinking about what we have learned today. If you want to stay behind and practice a bit more you can; otherwise, you can go to your workstations.

Figure 7.49 Lesson Close

Close
◆ What did we do today? ◆ What was the math we were practicing? ◆ What were we doing with our pattern blocks? ◆ Was this easy or tricky? ◆ Are there any questions?

Figure 7.50 Visual Introduction

Introduction to Visual Explorations

Launch	**Teacher:** Today we are going to work on dividing fractions with sketches.
	Vocabulary: halves, thirds, fourths, fifths, sixths, eighths, tenths, twelfths, denominator, numerator, whole number, dividend, divisor, quotient
	Math Talk: I divided ___ by ___. The quotient is ____.
Model	**Teacher:** Listen I am going to tell you a story. Grandma Betsy made a cake. She cut it into sixths. How many pieces did she get? (Teacher gives time for students to work on it.) Turn and explain what you did to your partner, and then be ready to share.
	Taylor: 6/6 makes 1 whole. If you cut the cake into sixths, then 6 of the sixths makes a whole.

Figure 7.50 (Continued)

Introduction to Visual Explorations

Checking for Understanding	**Teacher:** Listen I am going to tell you a story. Grandma Betsy made 2 cakes. She cut them into thirds. How many pieces did she get? **Let's explore.** **Here is 1/3.** **How many of these can we take out of this?** **Michael:** She got 3 pieces out of each cake. So if she had 2 cakes, she got 6 pieces. **Here is the cake:**  **Teacher:** Okay, you are going to each work on a problem and model it. You will share your work with your buddy, and then be ready to come back to the group and share with us all.

Figure 7.51 Visual Student Activity

Visual Student Activity	
Guided Practice/ Checking for Understanding	**Teacher:** Mike, tell me what you are doing? **Michelle:** I had 4 divided by 1/4. I know that 4/4 makes 1 whole so I have to multiply 4 × 4, and that is 16. So I got 16 pieces of cake. 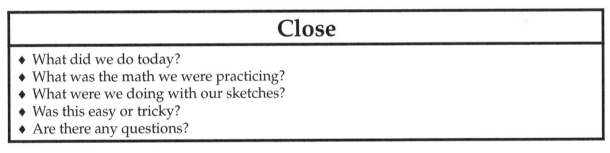
Set Up for Independent Practice	**Teacher:** Okay, turn and tell your neighbor what you are thinking about what we have learned today. If you want to stay behind and practice a bit more you can; otherwise, you can go to your workstations.

Figure 7.52 Lesson Close

Close
◆ What did we do today? ◆ What was the math we were practicing? ◆ What were we doing with our sketches? ◆ Was this easy or tricky? ◆ Are there any questions?

Figure 7.53 Abstract Introduction

Introduction to Abstract Explorations

Launch	**Teacher:** Today we are going to work on dividing fractions with a board game.

Vocabulary: halves, thirds, fourths, fifths, sixths, eighths, tenths, twelfths, denominator, numerator, whole number, dividend, divisor, quotient

Math Talk:
I divided ___ by___. The quotient is ____.

Teacher: Here is the board game. The problems on it are division problems. So you spin, land on a problem and solve it. If you are correct, you stay there. If you are incorrect, you have to go back a space. Whoever reaches finish first wins. Are there any questions about how to play? Also, who can explain the procedure for dividing fractions?

Dividing Fractions by a Whole Number:

Instructions: Spin the spinner. Whoever has the lowest number goes first. Move that many spaces and solve the problem where you land. The first person to land on finish wins.

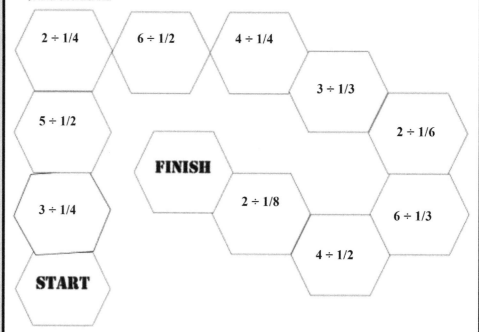

Martin: I can. You put the whole number over 1, and you flip the other factor.

Introduction to Abstract Explorations	
Model	**Teacher:** Who can explain the concept? What are we doing when we are dividing fractions? **Mary:** I can. You are partitioning the whole into a certain number of pieces.
Checking for Understanding	**Teacher:** So, if I landed on 2 divided by 1/4, what would the answer be? **Todd:** The answer would be 8. **Teacher:** Who agrees? (All the students nod their heads in agreement).

Figure 7.54 Abstract Student Activity

Abstract Student Activity	
Guided Practice/ Checking for Understanding	**Teacher:** You all are going to play the game in groups of 2s or 3s. I am going to watch, take some notes and ask you some questions. **Teacher:** Kelli and Mike, tell me about a problem that each of you solved so far. **Kellie:** The problem I solved is 5 divided by 1/2, and I got 10. **Mike:** The problem I solved is 2 divided by 1/3, and I got 6.
Set Up for Independent Practice	**Teacher:** Okay, as we end the session, turn and tell your neighbor what you are thinking about what we have practiced today. If you want to stay behind and practice a bit more you can; otherwise, you can go to your workstations.

Figure 7.55 Lesson Close

Close
◆ What did we do today?
◆ What was the math we were practicing?
◆ What were we doing with our board game?
◆ Was this easy or tricky?
◆ Are there any questions?

Section Summary

Dividing fractions is so much more than "flip it and multiply." It is important to spend time building conceptual understanding of this concept. Students should tell stories of dividing fractions by whole numbers and dividing whole numbers by fractions. Dividing fractions by whole numbers tends to be more complicated for students to understand. Don't rush it. Tell lots of stories. Students should have to not only solve problems but also make them up so that it is clear that they understand what the expressions mean. Students should also have to sketch out their models and explain the expressions.

Depth of Knowledge

Depth of Knowledge (DoK) is a framework that encourages us to ask questions that require that students think, reason, explain, defend and justify their thinking (Webb, 2002). Here is snapshot of what that can look like in terms of fraction work.

Figure 7.56 DoK Activities

	What are different ways to add fractions with unlike denominators?	What are different ways to subtract fractions with unlike denominators?	What are different ways to multiply a fraction by a fraction?	What are different ways to divide whole numbers and fractions?
DoK Level 1 (These are questions that require students to simply recall/ reproduce an answer/do a procedure.)	Solve: 1/4 + 1/2	Solve: 7/8 – 2/4	Solve: 1/2 × 1/2	Solve: $9 \div 1/3 =?$
DoK Level 2 (These are questions that have students use information, think about concepts and reason. This is considered a more challenging problem than a level 1 problem.)	Solve: 1/4 + 1/2 Solve: 2/6 + ? = 8/12 Explain your thinking. Model in 2 different ways.	Solve: 7/8 – 2/4 Solve: 7/8 – ? = 2/4 Explain your thinking. Model in 2 different ways.	Solve: 1/2 × 1/2 Explain your thinking. Model in 2 different ways.	Solve: $9 \div 1/3 =?$ Solve: $1/3 \div 3$ Explain your thinking. Model in 2 different ways.
DoK Level 3 (These are questions that have students reason, plan, explain, justify and defend their thinking)	Write your own fraction addition problem with unlike denominators. Explain your thinking and model your answer in 2 different ways.	Write your own fraction subtraction problem with unlike denominators. Explain your thinking and model your answer in 2 different ways.	The answer is 1/2. Tell me 2 multiplication expressions that will give this answer.	Pick a whole number and a fraction. Make a fraction division problem and explain your answer with numbers, words and pictures.

Adapted from Kaplinsky (https://robertkaplinsky.com/depth-knowledge-matrix-elementary-math/). A great resource for asking open questions is Marion Small's *Good Questions: Great Ways to Differentiate Mathematics Instruction in the Standards-Based Classroom* (2017).

Also Robert Kaplinsky has done a great job in pushing our thinking forward with the DoK matrices he created. The Kentucky Department of Education also has a great DoK math matrix (2007).

Figure 7.57 Asking rigorous questions

DoK 1	DoK 2 **At this level students explain their thinking.**	DoK 3 **At this level students have to justify, defend and prove their thinking with objects, drawings and diagrams.**
What is the answer to . . . Can you model the number? Can you model the problem? Can you identify the answer that matches this equation?	How do you know that the equation is correct? Can you pick the correct answer and explain why it is correct? How can you model that problem? What is another way to model that problem? Can you model that on the . . . Give me an example of a . . . type of problem. Which answer is incorrect? Explain your thinking?	Can you prove that your answer is correct? Prove that . . . Explain why that is the answer . . . Convince me that . . . Defend your thinking.

Key Points

♦ Adding Fractions With Unlike Denominators
♦ Subtracting Fractions With Unlike Denominators
♦ Multiplying Fractions
♦ Dividing Fractions and Whole Numbers

Chapter Summary

Teaching fractions in 5th grade is very important. The work starts in the lower elementary grades, but it is much more formal in 3rd, 4th and 5th grades. For students to really grasp the topics they must be introduced at the concrete level. Many textbooks go straight to pictorial representations, but students need plenty of opportunities to manipulate the models. They should use commercial ones, but they should also make their own individual sets of fraction squares, strips and circles. For the circles, it is best to cut out the paper copies so they are sure to be equal parts. Next, students should work on drawing their representations. This takes it to the next level of ownership of the internal knowledge of fractions. Throughout the process teachers should make explicit connections between the three representations of concrete, pictorial and abstract. Do not rush to the symbolic representation. Teach fractions all year long through routines and energizers. At the beginning of the year, be sure to do energizers and routines with the concepts they learned in the prior grades.

Reflection Questions

1. How are you currently teaching fraction lessons?
2. Are you making sure that you do concrete, pictorial and abstract activities?
3. What do your students struggle with the most, and what ideas are you taking away from this chapter that might inform your work?

References

Empson, S. B. (1999). Equal Sharing and Shared Meaning: The Development of Fraction Concepts in a First-Grade Classroom. *Cognition and Instruction*, 17, 283–342.

Fazio, L., & Siegler, R. (n.d.). Teaching Fractions. *International Academy of Education & International Bureau of Education*.

Kentucky Department of Education. (2007). Support Materials for Core Content for Assessment Version 4.1 Mathematics. Retrieved on January 15, 2017, from the internet.

Maelasari, E., & Jupri, A. (2017). Analysis of Student Errors on Division of Fractions. *IOP Conference Series: Journal of Physics: Conference Series*, 812, 012033 Retrieved on January 25, 2021.

National Council of Teachers of Mathematics. (2007). *The Learning of Mathematics: 69th NCTM Yearbook*. Reston, VA: National Council of Teachers of Mathematics.

NCTM Session 10319 Retrieved on June 25, 2021, from https://nctm.confex.com/nctm/2012RP/webprogram/Session10319.html.

Smalls, M. (2017). *Good Questions: Great Ways to Differentiate Mathematics Instructions* (3rd edition). New York: TC Press.

Vamvakoussi, X., & Vosniadou, S. (2010). How Many Decimals Are Therebetween Two Fractions? Aspects of Secondary School Students' Understanding of Rational Numbers and Their Notation. *Cognition and Instruction*, 28(2), 181–209.

Webb, N. (2002). An Analysis of the Alignment between Mathematics Standards and Assessments for Three States. Paper Presented at the Annual Meeting of the American Educational Research Association, New Orleans, LA.

8

Decimal Guided Math Lessons

One day I was walking by a 5th-grade class in the South Bronx, and the teacher called me in the classroom to help with a decimal lesson. He was teaching a lesson out of the textbook about knitting and decimals. Everybody was confused, including me. So, he said, "Anytime you want to step in, Dr. Nicki," to which I replied, "Okay, but I'm not touching the problem on the board. I just want to talk to the students."

So, I gathered the students together on the rug, and I started asking them about their morning stop at the neighborhood bodega (local deli/mini market) that is next door to the school. Everyone goes into the bodega in the morning. Money or not. Just to look, smell, see, talk, and sometimes buy stuff. I began to present to the children scenarios that were familiar to them about buying items from the bodega in the morning. I asked if they had $5.00 how many egg sandwiches could they buy? How much change would they have left over? How much the small bag of potato chips cost, and how many they could buy if they cost a quarter? All the kids calculated the answers, in very different ways. It was amazing. Then, later we presented the algorithm. If I had my way, I would have kept doing real life (meaning situations from their lives), longer before introducing the traditional algorithm.

My point is that students need to be able to make sense of the math they are doing in realistic ways. One of the best ways to teach decimals is to gather up the local flyers from the restaurants where students eat, the stores where they shop and the sports they watch and then talk about the ways in which we see and use decimals in our everyday lives. See the idea of "real life" problems should be based in the "real lives" of the students we teach. We don't grow cornfields in the South Bronx. What I mean by that is that start where you are. Then teach about the cornfields in Nebraska, and all sorts of other problems, once students have the conceptual and contextual understanding then the procedural understanding flows more easily.

In 4th grade, students are introduced to decimals. They learn about tenths and hundredths and how to compare and add them. In 5th grade, it is like just jumping in the pool feet first. Students are expected to learn how to add, subtract, multiply, divide, compare, round and know everything about decimals. Of course, this is an introduction, because in most states it is not a fluency until 6th grade! Whew! I was scared there for a minute. But look at that, we only have to be introduced to ALL these things, not master them yet. The point here is that we have to take it slow and easy and make sure students understand the math.

It is very important to use concrete and pictorial models to develop deep understanding of decimals (NCTM, 2000). We need to think about decimals in terms of (1) real-world situations, (2) manipulatives, (3) pictures, (4) spoken symbols and (5) written symbols (Cramer, 2003). Students need to be able to move back and forth between these models and relate them to each other.

DOI: 10.4324/9781003169666-8

Research Note

Appropriate concrete and pictorial models allow students to construct meaning for rational numbers and operations with numbers. To develop deep understanding of rational number, 6th through 8th graders must experience a variety of models (NCTM, 2000 cited in Cramer, Monson, Wyberg, Leavitt, & Whitney, 2009) to which I would add, k-5 too.

Figure 8.1 Overview

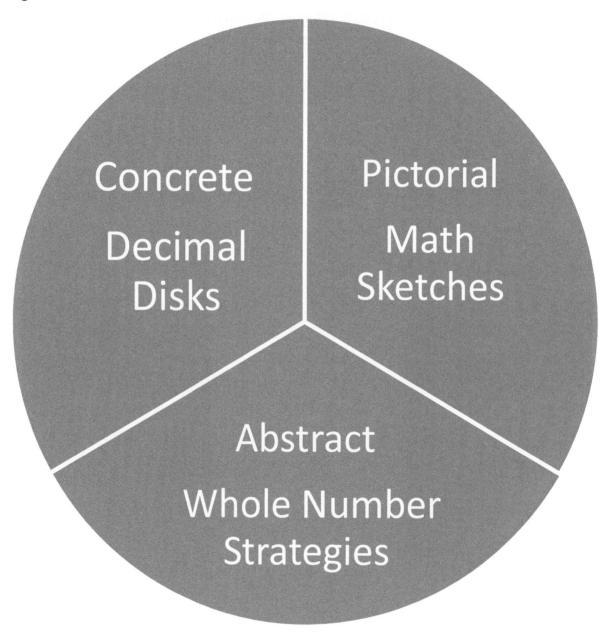

Figure 8.2 Planning Template

Adding Decimals

Big Idea: Numbers, Equivalence, Operation Meanings and Relationships **Enduring Understanding:** Students will understand that adding decimals can be modeled in many different ways. **Essential Question:** Why are decimals important? How do we use them in real life? **I can statement:** I can add decimals using many different models.	**Materials** ♦ Tools: Decimal Strips, decimal disks ♦ Templates: Decimal Strip Template ♦ Crayons, Pencils ♦ Paper

Cycle of Engagement

Concrete:

Pictorial:

.18 + .18 = .36

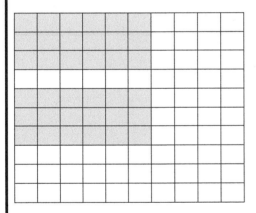

Abstract:

.35 + .22 = .57

Vocabulary & Language Frames

Vocabulary: decimals, tenths, hundredths, thousandths, whole number, sum, addends

Math Talk:
I added ___ and ___. My sum is ____.

Math Processes/Practices
♦ Problem-Solving
♦ Reasoning
♦ Models
♦ Tools
♦ Precision
♦ Structure
♦ Pattern

Pictorial:

1							
.50				.50			
.33‾			.33‾			.33‾	
.25		.25		.25		.25	
.166‾	.166‾	.166‾	.166‾	.166‾	.166‾		
.20		.20		.20		.20	.20
.125	.125	.125	.125	.125	.125	.125	.125

Figure 8.3 Differentiation

3 Differentiated Lessons		
In this series of lessons, students are working on adding decimals. They are developing this concept through concrete activities, pictorial activities and abstract activities. Here are some things to think about as you do these lessons.		
Emerging	**On Grade Level**	**Above Grade Level**
Do a lot of work with students looking at decimal grids and strips, charts and number lines. At the beginning of 5th grade, be sure to review all the 4th-grade decimal work. Start the year by doing a decimal-of-the-day routine that is continued throughout the year, adding components as the students learn them.	Do a lot of work with different manipulatives. Fifth grade is a foundational grade for decimal work because students learn to add, subtract, multiply and divide decimals, as well as round them. All students should have a decimal toolkit to help scaffold their thinking.	You can extend the number range. You can also have students work on an extended project where they explore decimals in real life. Also, give them an opportunity to teach about decimals using 21st-century technologies, such as blogs, podcasts, screencasts, SchoolTube videos, etc.

 Looking for Misunderstandings and Common Errors

Decimals are tricky. Be sure to use decimal tiles, decimal grids, decimal wheels, place-value disks and decimal number charts. These tools give students the opportunity to scaffold their learning concretely, pictorially and abstractly. Students often try to work with decimals by remembering rules rather than reasoning about them. Put the focus on reasoning and working with real-life situations where they are operating on decimals.

Figure 8.4 Anchor Chart

Concrete: 1.11 + .30 = 1.41

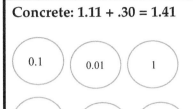

Pictorial:
.30 + .18 = .48

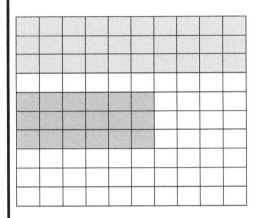

Abstract
.33 + .52 =.85
.3 + .5 = .8
.03 + .02 =.05
.80 + .05 = .85

Figure 8.5 Concrete Introduction

|	**Introduction to Concrete Explorations**
Launch	**Teacher:** Today we are going to work on adding decimals with place-value disks. **Vocabulary:** decimals, tenths, hundredths, thousands, whole number, sum, addends **Math Talk:** I added ___ and ___. My sum is ____.
Model	**Teacher:** Everyone has a baggie with place-value disks and a place-value mat. We are going to practice adding decimals with these tools. Let's add .55 and .33. Who can explain this model?  **Terri:** I see 5 tenths and 3 tenths, and that makes 8 tenths. And then there is a total of 8 hundredths. That would be .88 hundredths total.
Checking for Understanding	**Teacher:** Let's add .38 and .45. (Everyone models this, and they discuss the model). I am going to give each one of you sets of problems to explore. Then, we will go around, and each of you will pick a problem to share.

Figure 8.7 Lesson Close

	Concrete Student Activity
Guided Practice/ Checking for Understanding	**Teacher:** Marcos share your work with us. **Marcos:** I pulled .57 and .19. I had 16 hundredths . . . so I had to regroup 10 of those to make 1 tenth. And so I had 6 hundredths and 7 tenths. The answer is .76 hundredths.
Set Up for Independent Practice	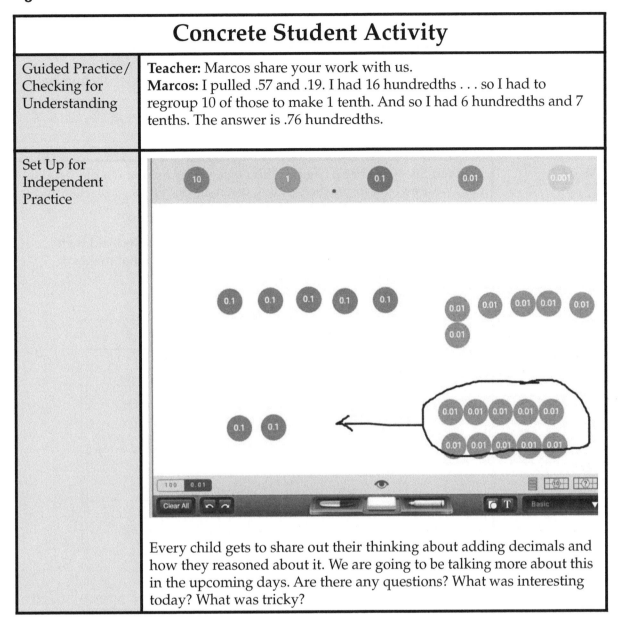 Every child gets to share out their thinking about adding decimals and how they reasoned about it. We are going to be talking more about this in the upcoming days. Are there any questions? What was interesting today? What was tricky?

Figure 8.6 Concrete Student Activity

Close
◆ What did we do today? ◆ What was the math we were practicing? ◆ What were we doing with our decimal disks? ◆ Was this easy or tricky? ◆ Are there any questions?

Figure 8.8 Visual Introduction

Introduction to Visual Explorations

Launch	**Teacher:** Today we are going to work on decimals with sketches. **Vocabulary:** decimals, tenths, hundredths, thousandths whole number, sum, addends **Math Talk:** I added ___ and ___. My sum is ____.
Model	**Teacher:** Everyone has a baggie with place-value disks and a place-value mat. We are going to practice adding decimals with these tools. Let's add .23 and .23. Who can draw it and explain this model? **Maria:** I see 2 tenths and 2 tenths and that makes 4 tenths. And then there is a total of 3 hundredths and 3 hundredths, and that makes 6 hundredths. That would be 46 hundredths total. 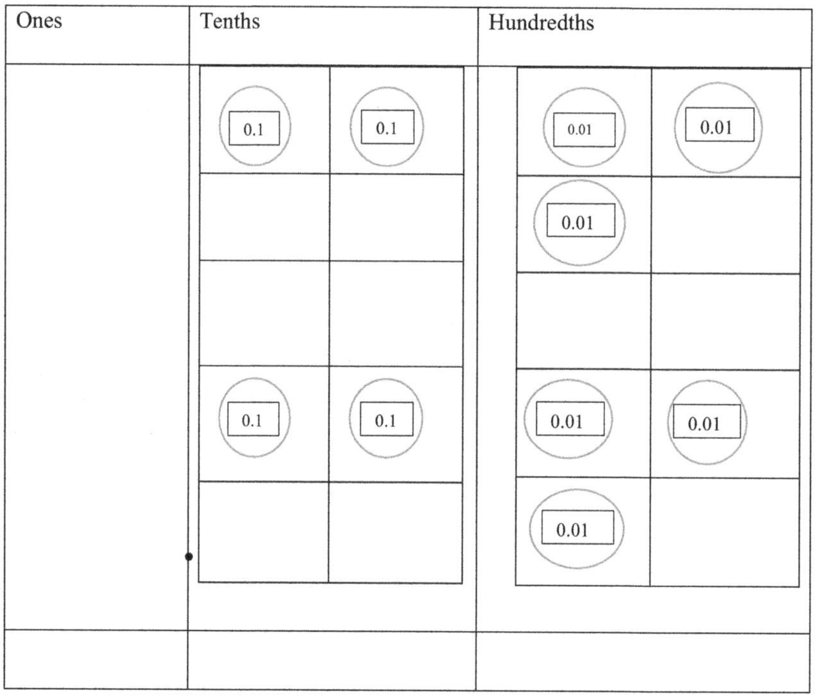 <table><tr><td>Ones</td><td>Tenths</td><td colspan="2">Hundredths</td></tr><tr><td></td><td>(0.1) (0.1)</td><td>(0.01)</td><td>(0.01)</td></tr><tr><td></td><td></td><td colspan="2">(0.01)</td></tr><tr><td></td><td>(0.1) (0.1)</td><td>(0.01)</td><td>(0.01)</td></tr><tr><td></td><td></td><td colspan="2">(0.01)</td></tr></table>
Checking for Understanding	**Teacher:** I want everyone to make up a problem where the sum is .67. (Everyone models this, and they discuss the model). I am going to give each one of you sets of problems to explore. Then, we will go around and each of you will pick a problem to share.

Figure 8.9 Visual Student Activity

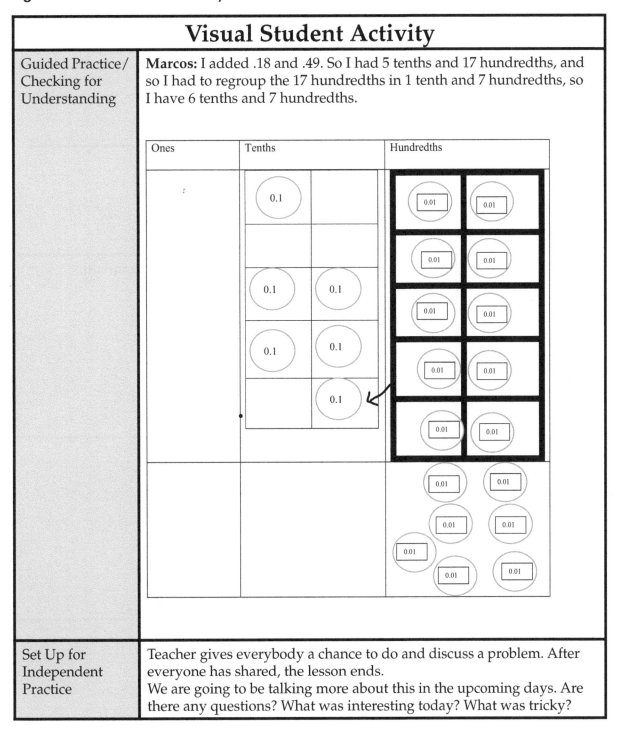

	Visual Student Activity	
Guided Practice/ Checking for Understanding	**Marcos:** I added .18 and .49. So I had 5 tenths and 17 hundredths, and so I had to regroup the 17 hundredths in 1 tenth and 7 hundredths, so I have 6 tenths and 7 hundredths.	
Set Up for Independent Practice	Teacher gives everybody a chance to do and discuss a problem. After everyone has shared, the lesson ends. We are going to be talking more about this in the upcoming days. Are there any questions? What was interesting today? What was tricky?	

Figure 8.10 Lesson Close

Close
♦ What did we do today?
♦ What was the math we were practicing?
♦ What were we doing with our sketches?
♦ Was this easy or tricky?
♦ Are there any questions?

Figure 8.11 Decimal Addition Template

Ones	⬤	Tenths	Hundredths

Work Area:

Sum:

Figure 8.12 Abstract Introduction

Introduction to Abstract Explorations

Launch	**Teacher:** Today we are going to work on adding decimals with the strategies that we use for whole numbers. **Vocabulary:** decimals, tenths, hundredths, thousands, whole number, sum, addends **Math Talk:** I added ___ and ___. My sum is ____.
Model	**Teacher:** Let's look at adding .59 and .22. What have we learned before that we could use here? **Sharon:** We could use the give-and-take strategy because we have a 9. So, we could make the .59 into .60 and the .22 into .21. Now we have an easier problem. The answer is .81. **Teacher:** Who agrees? Somebody explains what she just did. **Tom:** I agree. Whenever you see a 9, you should round it up because it will make the problem easier and you have to take one from the other addend to do it.
Checking for Understanding	**Teacher:** What is another way to think about this problem? **Kayla:** You could do partial sums. You could add the tenths, which would be .7, and then add the hundredths, which would be .11, and then we know that if it is over 10 that makes another tenth, and so we have 8 tenths and 1 hundredth. **Teacher:** Okay, I am going to give each of you a set of problems. I want you to work with your partner and think of strategies you could use to solve it. As you work, I am going to ask you all questions.

Figure 8.13 Abstract Student Activity

Abstract Student Activity	
Guided Practice/ Checking for Understanding	**Teacher:** Maya, tell me how you solved that problem. **Maya:** I had .77 and .8. So there is 15 tenths and 7 hundredths. But I know I have to take 10 tenths and make it a whole, so I have 1 whole 5 tenths and 7 hundredths. **Teacher:** Mike, what did you do? **Mike:** I had .34 and .52. I did partial sums. I added 8 tenths and then 6 hundredths. .86 is the answer.
Set Up for Independent Practice	**Teacher:** Okay, turn and tell your neighbor what you are thinking about what we have learned today. If you want to stay behind and practice a bit more you can; otherwise, you can go to your workstations.

Figure 8.14 Lesson Close

Close
♦ What did we do today?
♦ What was the math we were practicing?
♦ What were we doing with our whole number strategies?
♦ Was this easy or tricky?
♦ Are there any questions?

Section Summary

Adding decimals can be tricky, especially when the problems are written horizontally. Students have to really understand the importance of adding like parts. It goes way beyond "lining up the decimal." I think with the emphasis on partial sums students get to focus on the parts of the problem. Take the time to teach the concept with hands-on activities, and the students will remember it because they have done it. It is one thing to try to remember a random rule, and it is another to do math with understanding. Make sure that students can model their thinking in more than one way and that they can explain the expressions.

Subtracting Decimals

Figure 8.15 Overview

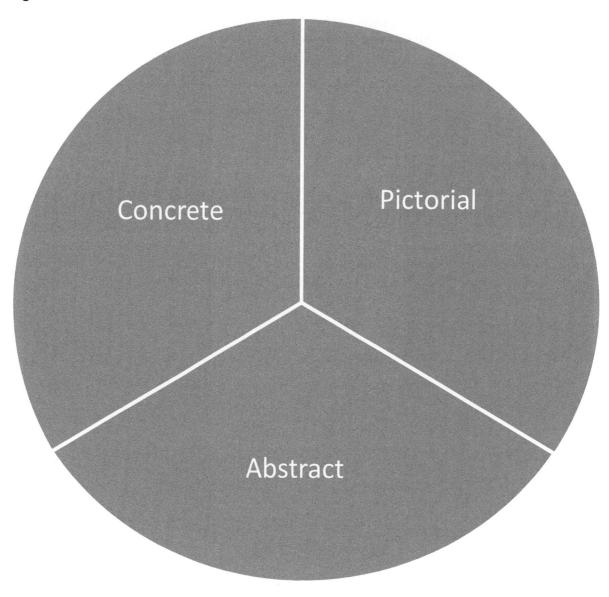

Figure 8.16 Planning Template

Subtracting Decimals

Big Idea: Numbers; Operation Meaning and Relationships **Enduring Understanding:** Students will understand how to subtract decimals. **Essential Question:** Why are decimals important? How do we use them in real life? **I can statement:** I can discuss and model subtracting decimals.	**Materials** ♦ Tools: Decimal Place-Value Disks ♦ Templates/Paper ♦ Crayons/Pencils

Cycle of Engagement

Concrete: .12 − .01 = .11

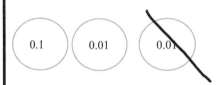

Pictorial:
.36 − .12 = .24

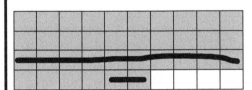

Abstract:
.35 − .22 = .13

Vocabulary & Language Frames

Vocabulary: ones, decimals, tenths, hundredths, thousands, whole number, minuend, subtrahend, difference, minus, take way, subtract

Math Talk:
I subtracted ___ from ___. My difference is ____.
My minuend is ____.
My subtrahend is ____.
My difference is ____.

Math Processes/Practices
♦ Problem-Solving
♦ Reasoning
♦ Models
♦ Tools
♦ Precision
♦ Structure
♦ Pattern

Figure 8.17 Differentiation

3 Differentiated Lessons

In this series of lessons, students are working on the concept of subtracting decimals. They are developing this concept through concrete activities, pictorial activities and abstract activities. Here are some things to think about as you do these lessons.

Emerging	On Grade Level	Above Grade Level
Students should review work with manipulatives to subtract decimals with like denominators. They should use decimal tiles, decimal wheels, decimal grids, place-value disks and decimal number charts to make connections from what they know to what they are doing on grade level. Review subtraction because many students have ongoing issues with subtraction.	Students should work with different models to subtract decimals. They should explore the concepts with money and lots of different other models.	You can extend the number range. You can also have students work on extended projects about decimals in real life.

 Looking for Misunderstandings and Common Errors

Decimals are tricky. Be sure to use decimal tiles, decimal grids, decimal wheels, place-value disks and decimal number charts. These tools give students the opportunity to scaffold their learning concretely, pictorially and abstractly. Students often try to work with decimals by remembering rules rather than reasoning about them. Put the focus on reasoning and working with real-life situations in which they are operating on decimals. As with many subtraction problems, have students think about counting up to the answer and about making friendly numbers to subtract through compensation strategies. Also do some intensive work on subtracting across zeros, mainly through strategies that make the numbers more friendly. Such as $4.00 take away $3.58. Students can think about counting up rather than trying to regroup across the zeros.

Figure 8.18 Anchor Chart

Concrete: .22 − .01 = .21

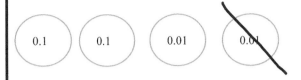

Pictorial:
.40 − .20 = .20

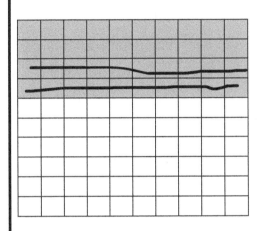

Abstract:
.35 − .22 = .13

Figure 8.19 Concrete Introduction

Introduction to Concrete Explorations

Launch	**Teacher:** Today we are going to work on subtracting decimals. **Vocabulary:** ones, decimals, tenths, hundredths, thousands, whole number, minuend, subtrahend, difference, minus, take way, subtract **Math Talk:** I subtracted ___ from ___. My difference is ____.
Model	**Teacher:** Everyone has a baggie with place-value disks and a place-value mat. We are going to practice subtracting decimals with these tools. Let's subtract .25 from .47. Who can explain this model? **Terri:** There was .47. I subtracted 2 tenths and 5 hundredths. I have 2 tenths and 2 hundredths left. *(place-value disk diagram: left group — 0.1, 0.1, 0.01, 0.01; right group — 0.01, 0.1, 0.01, 0.01, 0.1, 0.01)*
Checking for Understanding	**Teacher:** I am going to give each one of you sets of problems to explore. Then, we will go around and each of you will pick a problem to share.

Figure 8.20 Concrete Student Activity

	Concrete Student Activity
Guided Practice/ Checking for Understanding	**Teacher:** Let's subtract .09 from .33. Who wants to explain their thinking? **Marvin:** Well I need more hundredths, so I have to break up one of the tenths. Then I took away 9 hundredths, and I have 2 tenths and 4 hundredths left. The answer is .24. 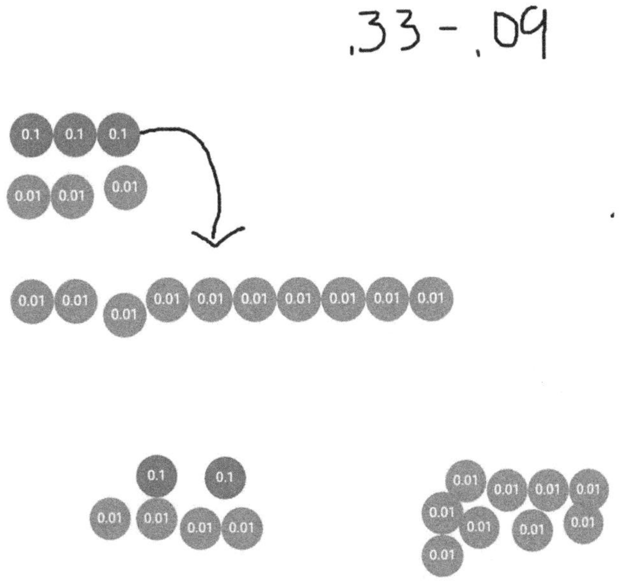 You could also just subtract a tenth and then add .01 back.
Set Up for Independent Practice	**Teacher:** Okay, turn and tell your neighbor what you are thinking about what we have learned today. If you want to stay behind and practice a bit more you can; otherwise, you can go to your workstations.

Figure 8.21 Lesson Close

Close
◆ What did we do today? ◆ What was the math we were practicing? ◆ What were we doing with our place-value disks? ◆ Was this easy or tricky? ◆ Are there any questions?

Figure 8.22 Visual Introduction

Introduction to a Visual Explorations

Launch	**Teacher:** Today we are going to work on subtracting decimals. **Vocabulary:** ones, decimals, tenths, hundredths, thousands, whole number, minuend, subtrahend, difference, minus, take way, subtract **Math Talk:** I subtracted ___ and ___. My difference is ____.
Model	**Teacher:** Everyone has a baggie with place-value disks and a place-value mat. We are going to practice subtracting decimals with these tools. Let's subtract .24 from .55. Who can explain this model? **Maria:** I took 2 tenths and 4 hundredths away. I have 3 tenths and 1 hundredth left. 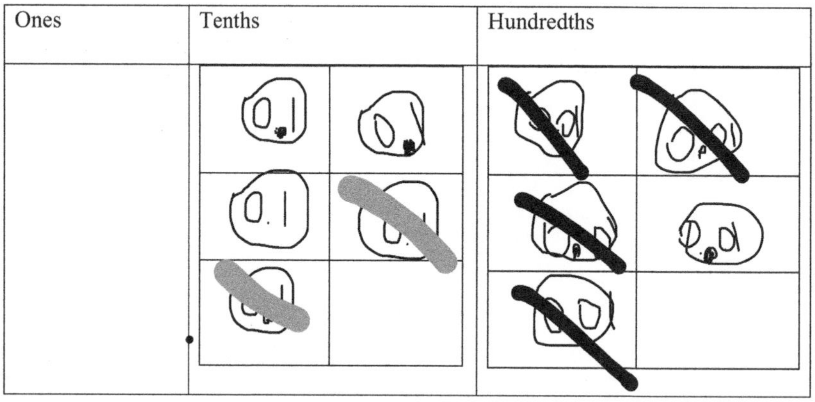
Checking for Understanding	**Teacher:** I am going to give each one of you sets of problems to explore. Then, we will go around and each of you will pick a problem to share.

Figure 8.23 Visual Student Activity

Visual Student Activity	
Guided Practice/ Checking for Understanding	**Teacher:** Who can explain what we are working on? **Tami:** We are subtracting decimals. **Teacher:** Everyone come up with a problem and model it. Then be ready to share your thinking. You can model it with any of the tools in your toolkit. **Yoli:** I did .75 − .34. So I started at .75, and I subtracted .30, and I got .45, and then I took away .04 more, and I got .41. <table><tr><td>.01</td><td>.02</td><td>.03</td><td>.04</td><td>.05</td><td>.06</td><td>.07</td><td>.08</td><td>.09</td><td>.10</td></tr><tr><td>.11</td><td>.12</td><td>.13</td><td>.14</td><td>.15</td><td>.16</td><td>.17</td><td>.18</td><td>.19</td><td>.20</td></tr><tr><td>.21</td><td>.22</td><td>.23</td><td>.24</td><td>.25</td><td>.26</td><td>.27</td><td>.28</td><td>.29</td><td>.30</td></tr><tr><td>.31</td><td>.32</td><td>.33</td><td>.34</td><td>.35</td><td>.36</td><td>.37</td><td>.38</td><td>.39</td><td>.40</td></tr><tr><td>.41</td><td>.42</td><td>.43</td><td>.44</td><td>.45</td><td>.46</td><td>.47</td><td>.48</td><td>.49</td><td>.50</td></tr><tr><td>.51</td><td>.52</td><td>.53</td><td>.54</td><td>.55</td><td>.56</td><td>.57</td><td>.58</td><td>.59</td><td>.60</td></tr><tr><td>.61</td><td>.62</td><td>.63</td><td>.64</td><td>.67</td><td>.66</td><td>.67</td><td>.68</td><td>.69</td><td>.70</td></tr><tr><td>.71</td><td>.72</td><td>.73</td><td>.74</td><td>.75</td><td>.76</td><td>.77</td><td>.78</td><td>.79</td><td>.80</td></tr><tr><td>.81</td><td>.82</td><td>.83</td><td>.84</td><td>.85</td><td>.86</td><td>.87</td><td>.88</td><td>.89</td><td>.90</td></tr><tr><td>.91</td><td>.92</td><td>.93</td><td>.94</td><td>.95</td><td>.96</td><td>.97</td><td>.98</td><td>.99</td><td>1.00</td></tr></table>
Set Up for Independent Practice	**Teacher:** Okay, turn and tell your neighbor what you are thinking about what we have learned today. If you want to stay behind and practice a bit more you can; otherwise, you can go to your workstations.

Figure 8.24 Lesson Close

Close
♦ What did we do today? ♦ What was the math we were practicing? ♦ What were we doing with our place-value disk sketches? ♦ Was this easy or tricky? ♦ Are there any questions?

Figure 8.25 Decimal Hundredths Grid

.01	.02	.03	.04	.05	.06	.07	.08	.09	.10
.11	.12	.13	.14	.15	.16	.17	.18	.19	.20
.21	.22	.23	.24	.25	.26	.27	.28	.29	.30
.31	.32	.33	.34	.35	.36	.37	.38	.39	.40
.41	.42	.43	.44	.45	.46	.47	.48	.49	.50
.51	.52	.53	.54	.55	.56	.57	.58	.59	.60
.61	.62	.63	.64	.67	.66	.67	.68	.69	.70
.71	.72	.73	.74	.75	.76	.77	.78	.79	.80
.81	.82	.83	.84	.85	.86	.87	.88	.89	.90
.91	.92	.93	.94	.95	.96	.97	.98	.99	1.00

Figure 8.26 Abstract Introduction

	Introduction to Abstract Lesson
Launch	**Teacher:** Today we are going to work on subtracting decimals with the strategies that we use for whole numbers. **Vocabulary:** ones, decimals, tenths, hundredths, thousands, whole number, minuend, subtrahend, difference, minus, take way, subtract **Math Talk:** I subtracted ___ from ___. The difference is ____. My strategy was _____.
Model	**Teacher:** Let's look at subtracting .58 and .29. What have we learned before that we could use here? **Sue:** We could use the make the problem easier strategy. We could add .01 to each number and make the problem .59 and .30. That is easy. **Teacher:** Who agrees? Somebody explains what she just did. **Todd:** I agree. Whenever you see a 9, you should round it up because it will make the problem easier, and you have to do the same thing to both numbers when you are subtracting.
Checking for Understanding	**Teacher:** What is another way to think about this problem? **Kayla:** You could count up. .01 is .30 and then jump .28 more, which gets you to .59. So that is a total jump of .29.

Figure 8.27 Abstract Student Activity

	Abstract Student Activity
Guided Practice/ Checking for Understanding	**Teacher**: Okay, I am going to give each of you a set of problems. I want you to work with your partner and think of strategies you could use to solve it. As you work, I am going to ask you all questions. **Teacher**: Magdelena, tell me how you solved that problem. **Magdelena:** I had .39 take away .14. I did partial differences. I took away the hundredths and got .05, and then I subtracted the tenths and got 2 tenths. The answer is .25. **Teacher:** Mike what did you do? **Mike:** I had .71 − .59 and I made an easier problem. I added .01 to each and got .72 − .60, and that makes .12.
Set Up for Independent Practice	**Teacher:** Okay, turn and tell your neighbor what you are thinking about what we have learned today. If you want to stay behind and practice a bit more you can; otherwise, you can go to your workstations. **Kiyana:** We worked on subtracting with different strategies. They are the same strategies we used for subtracting whole numbers.

Figure 8.28 Lesson Close

Close
◆ What did we do today? ◆ What was the math we were practicing? ◆ What were we doing with our whole number strategies? ◆ Was this easy or tricky? ◆ Are there any questions?

Section Summary

Subtracting decimals can be tricky, especially when the problems are written horizontally. Students have to really understand the importance of subtracting like parts and making exchanges when necessary. It goes way beyond "lining up the decimal." I think with the emphasis on partial differences, students get to focus on the parts of the problem. Take the time to teach the concept with hands-on activities, and the students will remember it because they have done it. It is one thing to try to remember a random rule, and it is another to do math with understanding. Make sure that students can model their thinking in more than one way and that they can explain the expressions.

Figure 8.29 Overview

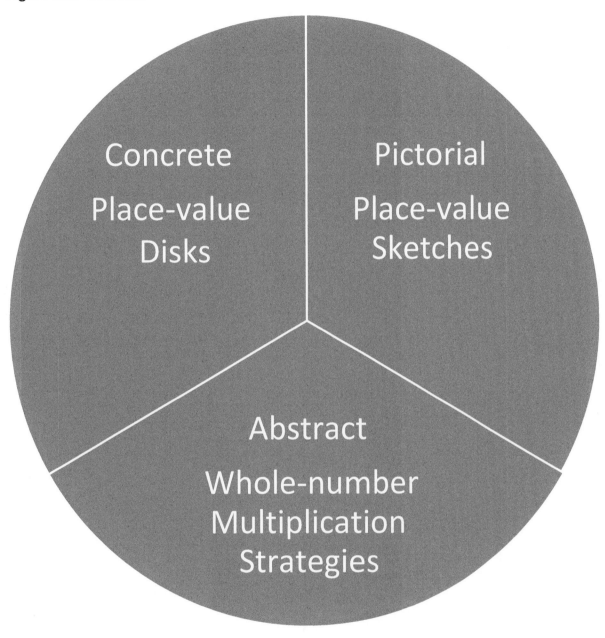

Figure 8.30 Planning Template

Multiplying Decimals

Big Idea: Numbers; Operation Meaning and Relationships **Enduring Understanding:** Students will understand how to multiply decimals. **Essential Question:** Why are decimals important? How do we use them in real life? **I can statement:** I can discuss and model multiplying decimals.	**Materials** ♦ Tools: Decimal Place-Value Strips ♦ Templates/Paper ♦ Crayons/Pencil

Cycle of Engagement

Concrete: $3 \times .10$

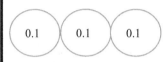

Pictorial: $3 \times .10$

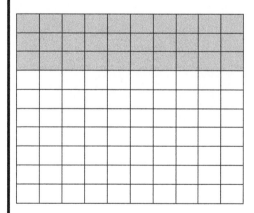

Abstract: $3 \times .10 = .30$

Vocabulary & Language Frames

Vocabulary: decimals, tenths, hundredths, thousands, whole number, factor, product, multiply

Math Talk:
I multiplied ___ and ___. The product is ___.

Math Processes/Practices
♦ Problem-Solving
♦ Reasoning
♦ Models
♦ Tools
♦ Precision
♦ Structure
♦ Pattern

Figure 8.31 Differentiation

3 Differentiated Lessons
In this series of lessons, students are working on understanding multiplying decimals. They are developing this concept through concrete activities, pictorial activities and abstract activities. Here are some things to think about as you do these lessons.

Emerging	On Grade Level	Above Grade Level
Students should work with different models starting with concrete manipulatives.	Students should discuss various strategies and use different models.	Students should work with larger decimals.

 Looking for Misunderstandings and Common Errors

Students often have trouble multiplying basic numbers, and this just gets more complicated with decimals. They often get confused. Remember: Decimals don't move. Numbers get larger or smaller but decimals don't move. Use decimal sliders and place value mats that students can stand in to act out the problems (see https://www.pinterest.com/drnicki7/decimals/act-it-out/)

Figure 8.32 Anchor Chart

Concrete:
Decimal Disks
Concrete: 4 × .10

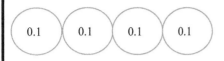

Pictorial: 6 × .05 = .30

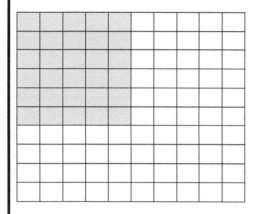

Abstract: 3 × .25 = .75
3 × .2 = 0.6
3 × .05 = .15
0.6 + .15 = .75

Figure 8.33 Concrete Introduction

Introduction to Concrete Explorations

Launch	**Teacher:** Today we are going to work on multiplying decimals **Vocabulary:** decimals, tenths, hundredths, thousands, whole number, factor, product, multiply **Math Talk:** I multiplied ___ and ___. The factors are ____. The product is _____.
Model	**Teacher:** Everyone has a baggie with place-value disks and a place-value mat. We are going to practice multiplying decimals with these tools. Let's multiply 4 × .25. Who can explain it with a model? **Trina:** I know the answer because it is 4 quarters. Here is what it looks like. It makes $1. 
Checking for Understanding	**Teacher:** Who can explain the idea of multiplying a whole number and decimals? **Carlton:** It is groups of something.

Figure 8.34 Student Concrete Activity

	Concrete Student Activity
Guided Practice/ Checking for Understanding	**Teacher:** Everyone has a decimal toolkit. We are going to practice multiplying decimals with these tools. Let's multiply .37 × 3. Everybody pick a way to model the problem. Do it and explain your thinking to your neighbor. Be ready to share your thinking with the group.
	Taylor: So I did 3 × .40 Then I knew that I had to subtract .09 because I put 3 too many in each group. So the answer would be 1.11.
Set Up for Independent Practice	**Teacher:** We are going to continue working on this during the next few weeks. What questions do you have for me?
	Yesenia: It is very tricky when we have to keep regrouping. I think that is very tricky. I get confused sometimes.
	Todd: Me too.
	Teacher: Okay, we will keep practicing doing that. We will get it for sure!

Figure 8.35 Lesson Close

Close
♦ What did we do today?   ♦ What was the math we were practicing?   ♦ What were we doing with our place-value disks and mats?   ♦ Was this easy or tricky?   ♦ Are there any questions?

Figure 8.36 Visual Introduction

Introduction to Visual Explorations

Launch	**Teacher:** Today we are going to work on multiplying decimals with place-value disks sketches. **Vocabulary:** decimals, tenths, hundredths, thousands, whole number, factor, product, multiply **Math Talk:** I multiplied ___ and ___. The factors are ___. The product is _____.
Model	**Teacher:** Everyone has a multiplication mat. We are going to practice multiplying a decimal and a whole number today. We will be looking at ___ groups of ____. Let's sketch out 4 × .15. **Trina:** I added up the tenths, and I got 4 tenths. I added up the hundredths, and I got 20 hundredths. I know that 20 hundredths is 2 more tenths. So I have 6 tenths. The answer is .6. 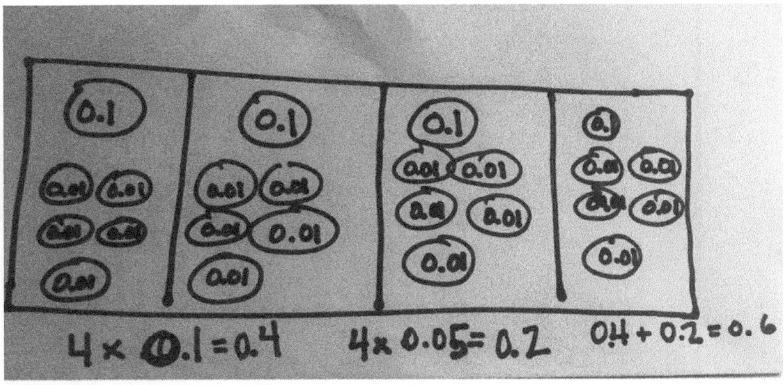
Checking for Understanding	**Teacher:** Who can explain the idea of multiplying a whole number and decimals? **Carlton:** It is groups of something. We can use different things to model our thinking. **Teacher:** Okay, I am going to give each one of you a problem. You are going to model it, share it with your shoulder buddy and then share your thinking with the group. While you are working, I might ask you some questions.

Figure 8.37 Visual Student Activity

<table>
<tr><th colspan="2" style="text-align:center;">Visual Student Activity</th></tr>
<tr>
<td>Guided Practice/
Checking for
Understanding</td>
<td>

Teacher: Teddy, tell me what you did.

Teddy: I had 2 × .10. I got 2 tenths. It is 2 groups of a tenth or 2 dimes.

Teacher: Who has another one?

Carla: I did .27 × 7. So I did quarter and pennies.

I did 7 quarters and then I had 7 × .02, which is another 14 cents. So I added it and it is $1.89.

</td>
</tr>
<tr>
<td>Set Up for
Independent
Practice</td>
<td>

Teacher: We are going to continue working on this during the next few weeks. What questions do you have for me?

Yesenia: It is very tricky when we have to keep regrouping. I think that is very tricky. I get confused sometimes.

Todd: Me too.

Teacher: Okay, we will keep practicing doing that. We will get it for sure!

</td>
</tr>
</table>

Figure 8.38 Lesson Close

Close
◆ What did we do today? ◆ What was the math we were practicing? ◆ What were we doing with our place-value mat sketches? ◆ Was this easy or tricky? ◆ Are there any questions?

Figure 8.39 Abstract Introduction

Introduction to Abstract Explorations	
Launch	**Teacher:** Today we are going to work on multiplying decimals with the strategies that we use for whole numbers. **Vocabulary:** decimals, tenths, hundredths, thousands, whole number, factor, product, multiply **Math Talk:** I multiplied ___ and ___. The product is ____. My strategy was _____.
Model	**Teacher:** Let's look at multiplying 3 × .49. Let's look at this problem. Think about it and share your thinking with a neighbor. Then, we will come back and talk about it together. **Raul:** I rounded .49 to 5 tenths because that makes it easy. It would be 1.50. But then I have to subtract 3 hundredths, and I get 1.47. **Marta:** I did the same thing. **Hong:** I did partial products. I did 3 × 4 tenths, which is 1 and 2 tenths, and then I multiplied 3 × .09, which is .27 hundredths, and I added that, and I got 1.47 hundredths.
Checking for Understanding	**Teacher:** Who can explain the concept of multiplying decimals? **Marta:** It is like adding the decimal that many times. **Teacher:** Is there just one way to do it? **Ted:** No, there are lots of ways to think about it using the same strategies we use for regular multiplication.

Figure 8.40 Abstract Student Activity

	Abstract Student Activity
Guided Practice/ Checking for Understanding	**Teacher:** Okay, so what are we thinking about multiplying decimals by whole numbers? **Tami:** That you can use different multiplication strategies to do it. **Teacher:** Okay, I am going to give you different problems and you will work on them and share your thinking with your shoulder buddy. Then be prepared to share your thinking with the group. I am going to ask you questions as you work. **Teacher:** Kayla, tell me what you did. **Kayla:** I had 5 × .27. I thought about quarters. I know that it is 1.25 plus .10. So I get 1.35.
Set Up for Independent Practice	**Teacher:** Okay, share that with the group. Who has another way to think about that? **Ted:** I would do partial products too. I would do, 5 × .20, which is 1 whole, and then 5 × .07, which is .35, so I'd get 1.35. **Teacher:** We are going to continue to work on these problems. What was tricky **Carla:** It is tricky when you have to regroup. **Yesenia:** You just have to remember that if you go over 10 in any place, you have to regroup that to the next place. **Teacher:** Okay, we will work on these some more next time. If anybody has questions, you can stay, and I'll work with you. You can go to your workstations.

Figure 8.41 Lesson Close

Close
◆ What did we do today? ◆ What was the math we were practicing? ◆ What were we doing with our multiplication strategies? ◆ Was this easy or tricky? ◆ Are there any questions?

Section Summary

Multiplying decimals can be very tricky for students. Oftentimes, the problems that students have with multidigit multiplication carry over into multiplication with decimals. Take the time to teach the concept with hands-on activities, and the students will remember it because they have done it. It is one thing to try to remember a random rule, and it is another to do math with understanding. Make sure that students can model their thinking in more than one way and that they can explain the expressions.

Dividing Decimals

Figure 8.42 Overview

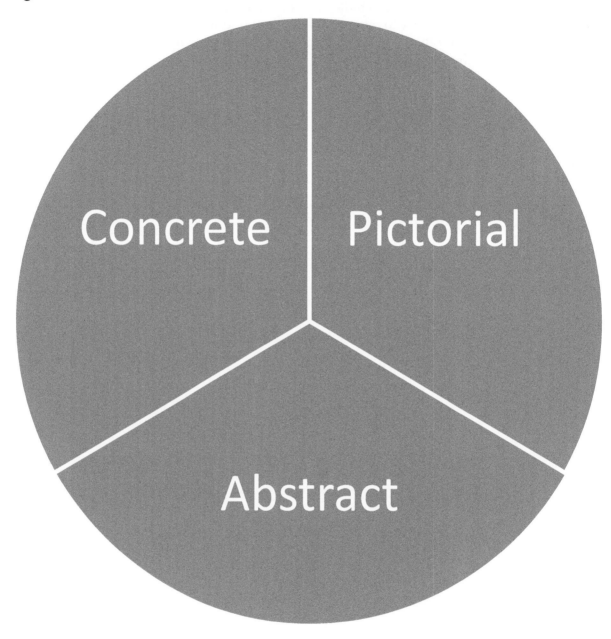

Figure 8.43 Planning Template

Dividing Decimals	
Big Idea: Numbers; Operation Meaning and Relationships **Enduring Understanding:** Students will understand how to divide fractions with whole numbers. **Essential Question:** Why are decimals important? How do we use them in real life? **I can statement:** I can discuss and model dividing decimals.	**Materials** ♦ Tools: Decimal Place-Value Disks ♦ Templates/Paper ♦ Crayons/Pencils ♦ Paper

Cycle of Engagement

Concrete: .40 ÷ 2 = .20

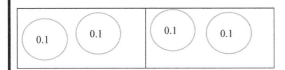

Pictorial: .12 ÷ 3 = .04

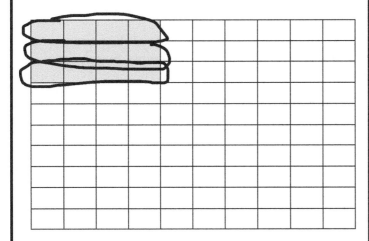

Abstract:
.12 ÷ 3 = .04

Vocabulary & Language Frames

Teacher: Today we are going to work on dividing decimals with place-value disks.
Vocabulary: decimals, tenths, hundredths, thousands, whole number, divisor, dividend, quotient, divide
Math Talk:
I divided ___ by ___. The divisor is _____. The dividend is _____. The quotient is _____.

Math Processes/Practices
♦ Problem-Solving
♦ Reasoning
♦ Models
♦ Tools
♦ Precision
♦ Structure
♦ Pattern

Figure 8.44 Differentiation

3 Differentiated Lessons

In this series of lessons, students are working on understanding dividing decimals. They are developing this concept through concrete activities, pictorial activities and abstract activities. Here are some things to think about as you do these lessons.

Emerging	On Grade Level	Above Grade Level
Students should work with different models. Be sure to review dividing within 100 and then dividing double-, triple- and quadruple-digit numbers by a single-digit divisor. Many students are still very shaky on these prerequisite skills. Be sure to use concrete, pictorial and abstract models.	Students should use models to understand how to divide decimals. Remember that the traditional algorithm for division is a 6th-grade standard. You want students to be using various strategies for division. Students should be explaining what they are doing, and they should be discussing different strategies and models for the division of decimals.	Extend the number range. Also, have the students work on real-world explorations about decimal division. Getting them to demonstrate it with various models is also a great, mathematically rich, standards-based engaging project.

 Looking for Misunderstandings and Common Errors

Students have trouble with division in general. If the problem is written horizontally, they can't figure out which number goes where when they set it up in a traditional long division way. They also get confused about where to place the decimal. All the problems that students have with regular division are only multiplied with decimals because on top of those, students get confused about where to put the decimal. Remember that decimals don't move. Numbers get larger or smaller, but decimals don't move. The emphasis should be on reasoning about the numbers.

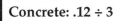

Figure 8.45 Anchor Chart

Concrete: .12 ÷ 3

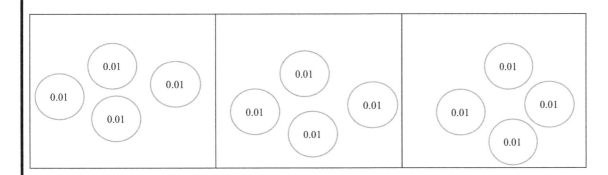

Pictorial: .20 ÷ 4 = .05

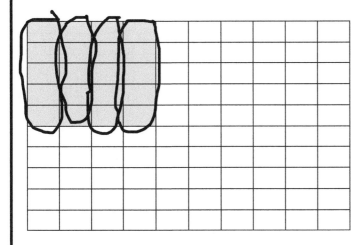

Abstract
.12 ÷ 3 = .04

Figure 8.46 Concrete Introduction

Introduction to Concrete Explorations

Launch	**Teacher:** Today we are going to work on dividing decimals with place-value disks. **Vocabulary:** decimals, tenths, hundredths, thousands, whole number, divisor, dividend, quotient, divide **Math Talk:** I divided ___ by ___. The divisor is _____. The dividend is _____. The quotient is _____.
Model	**Teacher:** Everyone has a baggie with place-value disks and a place-value mat. We are going to practice dividing decimals with these tools. Let's divide .45 by 4. Who can explain this model? **Trina:** I put out .45. Each person got .11, and there is a remainder of .01. 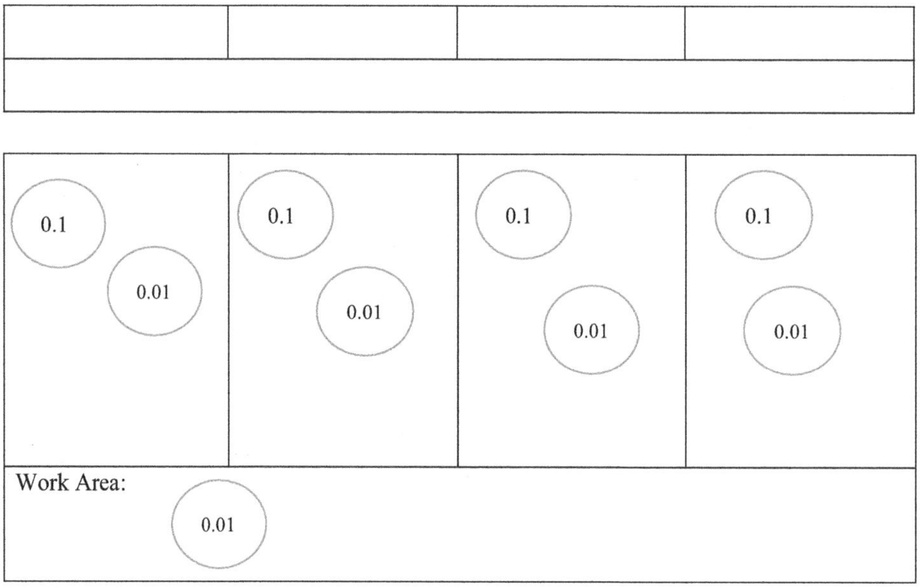

Checking for Understanding	**Teacher:** Who can explain the idea of dividing decimals and a whole number? **Carlton:** It is making equal groups. You have to find out how many of the group you can take out of the amount. So we can use the division mats to model our thinking. **Teacher:** Everyone has a baggie with place-value disks and a place-value mat. We are going to practice dividing decimals with these tools.

Figure 8.47 Student Concrete Activity

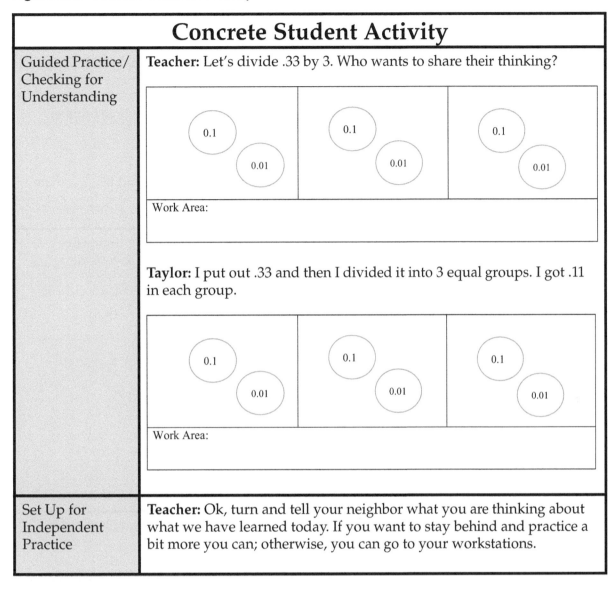

Concrete Student Activity	
Guided Practice/ Checking for Understanding	**Teacher:** Let's divide .33 by 3. Who wants to share their thinking?
	Taylor: I put out .33 and then I divided it into 3 equal groups. I got .11 in each group.
Set Up for Independent Practice	**Teacher:** Ok, turn and tell your neighbor what you are thinking about what we have learned today. If you want to stay behind and practice a bit more you can; otherwise, you can go to your workstations.

Figure 8.48 Lesson Close

Close
♦ What did we do today?
♦ What was the math we were practicing?
♦ What were we doing with our place-value disks?
♦ Was this easy or tricky?
♦ Are there any questions?

Figure 8.49 Visual Introduction

	Introduction to Visual Explorations
Launch	**Teacher:** Today we are going to work on dividing decimals with place-value disks and sketches. **Vocabulary:** decimals, tenths, hundredths, thousands, whole number, dividend, divisor, quotient, divide, division **Math Talk:** I divided ___ and ___. The divisor is _____. The dividend is _____. The quotient is _____.
Model	**Teacher:** Everyone has some division mats. We are going to practice dividing a decimal and a whole number today. We will be looking at ___ groups of ____. Let's sketch out .21 divided by 2. **Taylor:** I drew it, and I got .1, and there is a remainder of .01.
Checking for Understanding	**Teacher:** Who can explain the idea of dividing a whole number and decimals? **Hong:** Like if you have 50 cents and 2 people you would divide it among the 2 people. Each person would get $0.25. It's easy when you think about money. **Teacher:** Okay, I am going to give each one of you a problem. You are going to model it, share it with your shoulder buddy and then share your thinking with the group. While you are working, I might ask you some questions.

Figure 8.50 Visual Student Activity

Visual Student Activity	
Guided Practice/ Checking for Understanding	**Teacher:** Teddy, tell me what you did. **Teddy:** I had .27 divided by 5, and so I skip counted up to .25, and then there were 2 hundredths more. So it is 5 hundredths and a remainder of 2 hundredths.

.01	.02	.03	.04	05	.06	.07	.08	.09	.10
.11	.12	.13	.14	1	.16	.17	.18	.19	.20
.21	.22	.23	.24	25	.26	.27	.28	.29	.30
.31	.32	.33	.34	.35	.36	.37	.38	.39	.40
.41	.42	.43	.44	.45	.46	.47	.48	.49	.50
.51	.52	.53	.54	.55	.56	.57	.58	.59	.60
.61	.62	.63	.64	.67	.66	.67	.68	.69	.70
.71	.72	.73	.74	.75	.76	.77	.78	.79	.80
.81	.82	.83	.84	.85	.86	.87	.88	.89	.90
.91	.92	.93	.94	.95	.96	.97	.98	.99	1.00

Set Up for Independent Practice	**Teacher:** We are going to continue working on this during the next few weeks. What questions do you have for me? **Luke:** It is very tricky when we have to keep regrouping. I think that is very tricky. I get confused sometimes. **Jazmin:** I think when you think money it makes it easier. **Todd:** Me too. **Teacher:** Okay, we will keep practicing doing that. We will get it for sure! Anybody who has questions can stay and ask me. The rest of you can go to workstations.

Figure 8.51 Lesson Close

Close
◆ What did we do today? ◆ What was the math we were practicing? ◆ What were we doing with our division mats? ◆ Was this easy or tricky? ◆ Are there any questions?

Figure 8.52 Abstract Introduction

Introduction to Abstract Explorations

Launch	**Teacher:** Today we are going to work on dividing decimals using tools from our decimal kits if needed and strategies. **Vocabulary:** decimals, tenths, hundredths, thousands, whole number, dividend, divisor, quotient, divide, division **Math Talk:** I divided ___ by ___. The divisor is _____. The dividend is _____. The quotient is _____.
Model	**Teacher:** Today we are going to go around the group, and each person gets to tell a decimal division story. It can be about money, sports, or something else. Who wants to start? **Kayla:** I have a story. Mary went to the store. She had $2.00. She wanted to buy some potato chips. They cost $.50 each. How many can she buy? **Teacher:** Everybody take your time and figure out the problem. Then explain your thinking to your math buddy. Then we will share out. (After students have had time to share their thinking with each other, Tomas raises his hand.) **Tomas:** I know.50 and .50 make a $1. So if you can buy 2 bags with 1 dollar, then you can buy 4 bags with 2 dollars. **Carol:** I agree. **Teacher:** How might that look with symbols. Everybody do it on your whiteboards, discuss it with a partner and then we will discuss. *Students do it and then discuss the work.*
Checking for Understanding	**Teacher:** Who wants to go next? **Todd:** Grandma had $.75. She shared it with her 3 grandchildren. How much money did each kid get? **Lara:** 25 cents. 3 quarters make 75 cents. **Teacher:** Okay, everybody model your thinking with an equation too and show it to us on your whiteboards. *(Students do this.)*

Figure 8.53 Abstract Student Activity

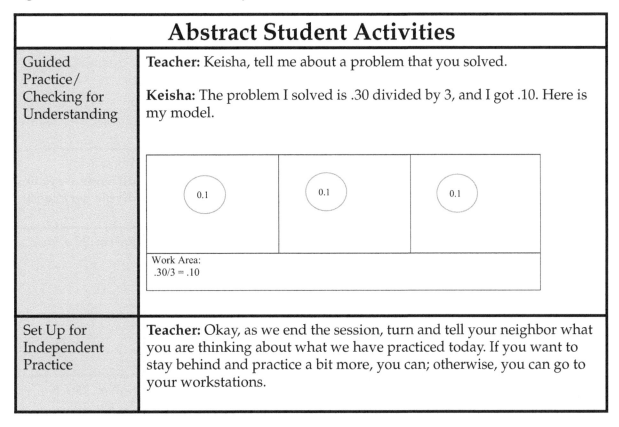

	Abstract Student Activities
Guided Practice/ Checking for Understanding	**Teacher:** Keisha, tell me about a problem that you solved. **Keisha:** The problem I solved is .30 divided by 3, and I got .10. Here is my model. Work Area: .30/3 = .10
Set Up for Independent Practice	**Teacher:** Okay, as we end the session, turn and tell your neighbor what you are thinking about what we have practiced today. If you want to stay behind and practice a bit more, you can; otherwise, you can go to your workstations.

Figure 8.54 Lesson Close

Close
◆ What did we do today? ◆ What was the math we were practicing? ◆ What were we doing with our division stories? ◆ Was this easy or tricky? ◆ Are there any questions?

Section Summary

Dividing decimals is challenging for many students. Like with other operations on decimals it is important for students to think about place and value rather than trying to just remember a rule about what happens with the decimal. It is important to use a variety of models and have students make sense between them. I have used place-value disks in these examples, but it is just as important to use grids and money.

Depth of Knowledge

Depth of Knowledge (DoK) is a framework that encourages us to ask questions that require students to think, reason, explain, defend and justify their thinking (Webb, 2002). Here is a snapshot of what that can look like in terms of place-value work.

Figure 8.55 DoK Activities

	What are different ways to add decimals?	What are different ways to subtract decimals?	What are different ways to multiply decimals?	What are different ways to divide decimals?
DoK Level 1 (These are questions that require students to simply recall/reproduce an answer/do a procedure.)	Solve: .45 + .57	Solve: .57 − .39	Solve: 4 × .25	Solve: .25 ÷ 5=
DoK Level 2 (These are questions that have students use information, think about concepts and reason. This is considered a more challenging problem than a Level 1 problem.)	Solve: .45 + .26 Solve: .45 + ? = .71 Explain your thinking and model your answer in 2 different ways.	Solve: .57 − .39 Solve: .57 − ? = .18 Explain your thinking and model your answer in 2 different ways.	Solve: 4 × .25 4 × ? = 1 Explain your thinking and model your answer in 2 different ways.	Solve: .25 ÷ 5= ? ÷ 4 = .10 Explain your thinking and model your answer in 2 different ways.
DoK Level 3 (These are questions that have students reason, plan, explain, justify and defend their thinking.)	Solve: The answer is .75. Tell me 2 addition expressions that will give me that answer.	Solve: The answer is .18. Tell me 2 subtraction expressions that will give me that answer.	The answer is .24. Tell me 2 multiplication expressions that will give me .24 as a product.	Pick a whole number and a decimal. Make a decimal division problem and explain your answer with numbers, words and pictures.

Adapted from Kaplinsky (https://robertkaplinsky.com/depth-knowledge-matrix-elementary-math/). A great resource for asking open questions is *Marion Small's Good Questions: Great Ways to Differentiate Mathematics Instruction in the Standards-Based Classroom* (2017).

Also, Robert Kaplinsky has done a great job in pushing our thinking forward with the DoK matrices he created. The Kentucky Department of Education also has a great DoK math matrix (2007).

Figure 8.56 Asking rigorous questions

DoK 1	DoK 2 At this level, students explain their thinking.	DoK 3 At this level, students have to justify, defend and prove their thinking with objects, drawings and diagrams.
What is the answer to . . . Can you model the number? Can you model the problem? Can you identify the answer that matches this equation?	How do you know that the equation is correct? Can you pick the correct answer and explain why it is correct? How can you model that problem? What is another way to model that problem? Can you model that on the . . . Give me an example of a . . . type of problem. Which answer is incorrect? Explain your thinking?	Can you prove that your answer is correct? Prove that . . . Explain why that is the answer . . . Convince me that . . . Defend your thinking.

Key Points

♦ Adding Decimals
♦ Subtracting Decimals
♦ Multiplying Decimals
♦ Dividing Decimals and Whole Numbers

Chapter Summary

Teaching decimals in 5th grade is very important. For students to really grasp the topics, they must be introduced at the concrete level. Many books go straight to pictorial representations, but students need plenty of opportunities to manipulate the models. Next, students should work on drawing their representations. This takes it to the next level of ownership of the internal knowledge of decimals. Finally, they should be doing abstract work with the symbols. Do not rush to the symbolic representation. Teach decimals all year long through routines and energizers. At the beginning of the year, be sure to do decimal energizers and routines with the concepts they learned in 4th grade.

Reflection Questions

1. How are you currently teaching decimals?
2. Are you making sure that you do concrete, pictorial and abstract activities?
3. What do your students struggle with the most, and what ideas are you taking away from this chapter that might inform your work?

References

Cramer, K. A. (2003). Using a Translation Model for Curriculum Development and Classroom Instruction. In R. Lesh & H. M. Doerr (Eds.), *Beyond Constructivisim: Models and Modeling Perspectives on MThematics Problem Solving, Learning and Teaching* (pp. 449–464). Mahwah, NJ: Lawrence Erlbaum Associates.

Cramer, K. A., Monson, D., Wyberg, T., Leavitt, S., & Whitney, S. (2009). Models for Initial Decimal Ideas. *Teaching Children Mathematics*, 16(2), 106–117. Retrieved on February 13, 2021, from www.jstor.org/stable/41199386.

Kentucky Department of Education. (2007). Support Materials for Core Content for Assessment Version 4.1 Mathematics. Retrieved on January 15, 2017, from the internet.

National Council of Teachers of Mathematics (NCTM). (2000). *Principles and Standards for School Mathematics*. Reston, VA: NCTM. *Curriculum Focal Points for Prekindergarten Through Grade 8 Mathematics: A Quest for Coherence*. Reston, VA: NCTM, 2006.

Smalls, M. (2017). *Good Questions: Great Ways to Differentiate Mathematics Instructions* (3rd edition). New York: TC Press.

Webb, N. (2002). An Analysis of the Alignment between Mathematics Standards and Assessments for Three States. Paper Presented at the Annual Meeting of the American Educational Research Association, New Orleans, LA.

9
Action Planning and FAQs

Well to get started, you must get started. Pick where you want to start and just begin. Begin small. Here is an Action Checklist (see Figure 9.1).

Figure 9.1 Action Checklist

Before the Lesson	
Decide on the topic that you want to do.	
Why are you doing this topic?	
Is this emerging, on grade level or advanced?	
Map out a 3-cycle connected lesson plan.	
What are you going to do concretely?	
What are you going to do pictorially?	
What are you going to do abstractly?	
What misconceptions and error patterns do you anticipate?	
During the Lesson	
What are your questions?	
How are the students doing?	
What do you notice?	
What do you hear?	
What do you see?	
After the Lesson	
What went well?	
What will you tweak?	
What will you do the same?	
What will you do differently?	

DOI: 10.4324/9781003169666-9 ♦

Figure 9.1 (Continued)

What made you say, "Wow?"	
What made you think, "Uh-oh . . ."?	
What did you notice?	
What did you wonder?	
Other Comments	

Frequently Asked Questions

1. **What is a guided math group?**
   Guided math is when you pull a temporary small group of students for instruction around a specific topic. Sometimes the groups are heterogeneous, and sometimes they are homogeneous. They depend on what you are teaching. If you are teaching a specific skill, like dividing fractions and you have some students who know it and others who are struggling, then sometimes you would pull the students who need further work exploring the topic into a small group. However, sometimes you are working on general concepts, like modeling with manipulatives or solving word problems with tape diagrams. You could pull a heterogeneous group to teach this.

2. **Why do guided math?**
   You do guided math for a variety of reasons. Lillian Katz said it best:

   > When a teacher tries to teach something to the entire class at the same time, chances are, one-third of the kids already know it; one-third will get it; and the remaining third won't. So two-thirds of the children are wasting their time.

   You do guided math so that everyone gets to learn. You can pull students to address relevant gaps, on-grade-level work and enrichment. You do guided math so that students understand the math they are doing. You work with students in small groups so that they can talk, understand, reason and do math!

3. **What are the types of lessons?**
   There are different types of guided math lessons: conceptual, procedural, reasoning, strategy and disposition. Mostly disposition lessons are integrated throughout the other lessons, but sometimes you just pull students and talk about their journey. That could look like, *"What is tricky about what we are learning?"* and *"What is easy?"*

4. **Do you always use manipulatives in a guided math group?**
   No. It depends on where you are in the cycle of developing the concepts and student understanding. You certainly should use manipulatives in the beginning when you are developing concepts, but eventually, when students are practicing at the abstract level, they probably won't be working directly with manipulatives. However, sometimes they will still use them to check their answers or even solve problems if they need to.

5. **What about doing worksheets in guided math groups?**
   Never. It's simple. Guided math is students doing math, not doing a worksheet. Sometimes, you do pull students to work on some specific problems on a journal page, but that is not the norm or the regular structure of a guided math group.

Reference

Katz, L. Retrieved on April 15, 2019, from www.azquotes.com/author/39264-Lilian_Katz.

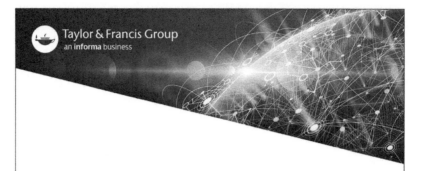